Paratroopers for Jesus
4,936 Band Name Suggestions From the '90s Internet

Edited by Andy Sturdevant

A Birchwood Palace publication
BP016

today's my super spaceout day

SALESMEN OF A DIVINE NATURE

BAND.COM IS A BAND.COM

Widows 95

ALGEBRA 2

Third edition, Fall 2024

Copyright © 2024 by Andy Sturdevant. All rights reserved.

Some names of actual existing bands have been removed and/or replaced since the second edition.

ISBN 979-8-9903187-0-0

Introduction edited by Sam Circle
www.lastweeksnewyorker.review

Data wrangling by Leah Puffer
Layout assistance by Ljiljana Pavkov

Cover image: "Van," by Daniel Lobo. Used under a CC0 1.0 Universal license.

Dedication page image: Photograph of Nate the Viking Featuring Dave courtesy of David R. Wolkensperg. All rights reserved.

Illustrations throughout are from the following Dover Publishing "Clip Art Series" publications: *Ready-to-Use Illustrations of Women's Heads,* by Tom Tierney, 1982; *Ready-To-Use Illustrations of Men's Heads,* by Tom Tierney, 1982; *Ready-To-Use Sports Illustrations,* by David Carlson, 1982; *Ready-to-Use School and Education Illustrations,* by Tom Tierney, 1987; *Ready-to-Use Office and Business Illustrations,* by Tom Tierney, 1988; *Ready-to-Use Illustrations of World-Famous Places,* by Charles Hogarth, 1993; *Illustrations of Appliances & Electronics,* by Sonny Schug, 1994.

Printed in Carver County, Minnesota, the traditional and contemporary homelands of the Sisseton and Wahpeton bands of the Dakhóta people. A percentage of Birchwood Palace Industries' annual revenue is contributed to Dakhóta language revitilization organizations in Minnesota.

Birchwood Palace Industries, L.L.C. is a publisher of artists books, zines and other small-run printed materials. It is a project of Andy Sturdevant, and is based in Minneapolis, Minnesota. Visit us on the World Wide Web at birchwoodpalace.com.

This book and the 4,936 band names within it are dedicated to the eternal memory of

Nate the Viking Featuring Dave

who were (and remain) banned from the Main Street Lounge for life.

Introduction
Andy Sturdevant

"That would be a great name for a rock band."

Yeah, it's a cliché, but in my youth, in the '90s and early aughts, this was the greatest compliment you could pay a turn of phrase. It was a defining refrain of the era, omnipresent in the band-adjacent circles I traveled through, but echoing everywhere in the culture. It was a staple of newspaper humorist Dave Barry's repertoire: "The Eerie Groin Legumes would be an excellent name for a rock band." Jon Stewart on *The Daily Show*: "If Lesbian Bondage Fiasco isn't the name of a hard-edged indie band by tomorrow, I'll be very disappointed." Zach Braff on *Scrubs*, when one character says their grandfather was killed in a seven-car pileup, another responds, "Seven Car Pile-Up would be a good name for a rock band." In college, I worked at an art supply store, and nearly every product we sold became a potential band name for me and my coworkers: *Das Pronto. Alizarin Crimson. Bone Folder.* (An Italian air-drying clay, oil paint pigment and bookmaking tool, respectively.) On slow days, the conversation would meander into easygoing pedantry: Obviously Das Pronto was a squad of take-action Gang of Four types, playing fast, sharp art-punk, while Bone Folder were a bunch of twee sadsacks, jangly guitars and wistful lyrics sung by a Kimya Dawson soundalike.

The romance of *being in a band* seeped into every facet of daily life. I knew a guy who said his solution to any problem was to take a deep breath, pick up a six-pack of beer, and start a band. Art critic Dave Hickey wrote that "the traveling band... exist[s] not just to preserve values, but to invent them, to propagate them by doing things in the world." You can't choose your family, but you can choose your bandmates, and if all goes well, you could all be driving around the United States together in an Econoliner van, sharing the joys and hardships of life on the road, your entire lives given over to camaraderie and creative expression. You and your band were bound together as comrades-in-arms, brothers and sisters fighting for a great and beautiful truth. (That's how we talked in those days.) After all, what could be more democratic than a band? All you really need, beyond the small matter of musical instruments and a basement in which to practice, is a good name. And anyone could come up with that. Even some dork on the internet.

It was in this context that I encountered the name Paratroopers for Jesus.

As a teenager, my two favorite things in the world were rock music and the internet. Each was a self-contained world, each a laboratory for identity formation. At the nexus of these two worlds, I scoured Yahoo! for any scraps of rock-related content I could find. On some long-forgotten .edu page, I found a List of Cool Band Names — and there it was, Paratroopers for Jesus. I was sixteen when I first read the name, and for thirty years it's followed me around. It wasn't a real band — not then, and not since. It was just a *name* for a band, a flippant suggestion. Perhaps it began as someone's inside joke, or a phrase overheard or misheard. Maybe it was a quip from some televangelist, maybe a sarcastic aside from a friend. Like a trace fossil, we can know the contours of whatever the joke was, though the organism is long gone. The phrase "Paratroopers for Jesus" is instantly evocative, calling to mind an entire visual identity cobbled together from all kinds of mid-century junk culture: *Sgt. Rock* comics, Chick tracts, the *National Enquirer,* Technicolor World War II movies, remaindered Jim Bakker memoirs. I can hear the music: Reverb-drenched guitars, heavy on the floor toms, absurdist lyrics about TV commercials and cat food. Mudhoney mixed with Man Or Astro-Man?, with a dash of Urge Overkill. A whole lifestyle, yours for the taking. To paraphrase the Minutemen, a band like that could be your life.

In 1996, Yahoo cataloged more than a dozen band-naming websites, hosted on GeoCities or college web servers, with names like "Official List of Stupid Band Names." They ran the gamut from sincere to absurd, and most solicited suggestions from site visitors. You the reader were encouraged to use any of them. Each one was an outline for a band you could start with two or three of your dirtbag friends. Along with the lists of choose-your-own-funny-band-names, some sites were created by unnamed bands who'd *already* formed, still needed a name, and solicited them in that most inefficient way of the pre-social media era: by building a website and waiting for the emails to roll in. One such group from Charlottesville, Virginia had a page at the extremely '90s URL www.cstone.net/~tmc. This page's presence on Yahoo!'s band naming directory drew a few dozen suggestions, but despite such high-quality contenders as Dr. Pornograffiti, Torture Club, and The Captain and Schlemiel, the members settled on the fairly anodyne alt-rock name *Juicebox*. Despite featuring members who'd worked with Charlottesville's favorite son, Dave Matthews, Juicebox seems to have vanished with little trace. If they'd called themselves The Great Unmaking or Atomic Mushroom, it might have been a different story.

The majority of band names in this book come from a PDF titled simply "band_names.pdf" that I found in 2023, tucked away as an unlabeled page on the website for the King Kongz School of Music in Townsville, in Queensland, Australia. Every few years, I'd Google the phrase "paratroopers for jesus," just to see what came up, to recover lost time, or just to confirm that my memory was actually true. For years, nothing came back. And then this PDF did. I did a Command-F for the name, and there it was, right between The Parameters and Parting Gift. Google still indexes pages that aren't directly linked, and while the King Kongz website where I found the document certainly wasn't the original home of this list (it predates the website), it hosts a copy of the file on the web, for reasons known but to God, or King Kong, or the guitar teachers who work there.

The origins of this source PDF are unclear and probably unknowable. The document's metadata gives us just a few vague clues. It was created by one Patrick Higgins at 10:46 a.m. on Thursday, March 23, 2006. It appears to be a compilation of four or five lists of band names. Higgins probably saved these lists from webpages, newsgroups, or forums, saving them as .txt files to his hard drive, copy-pasted sequentially in order of discovery. Some sections are alphabetized for pages at a time, others seem ordered at random. At some point he converted the list into a PDF with minimal formatting. (Thank god for the PDF, the most indestructible of digital formats.) Higgins was likely a music nerd of some kind, and there *is* a New York-based composer and guitarist by that name who'd be about the right age to have farted around on the web in the late '90s. That Patrick Higgins did not return a request for comment. The mystery remains.

Band-name lists were a product of their very specific moment in time, and by this PDF's creation in 2006, that moment was on the verge of passing. According to the Pew Research Center, 71% of U.S. adults used the internet that year, when this list was compiled, compared to 22% ten years earlier, when the entries on the list were created. The idea of the internet as a difficult-to-access playground for obsessives, programmers and academics with too much time on their hands was fading away, and Web 2.0 was dawning. Facebook was two years old, YouTube was one, and Twitter was still called *twttr*. In a few years, these sites would render webpage-based lists mostly obsolete: If you had a funny idea for a band name, you'd just tweet it or post it to your wall. The internet isn't eternal, and its epochs move quickly — many, maybe most, of the band-name sites built by land grant university undergrads or office drones vanished. They're deleted when their host gets her degree, quits her job, forgets to pay her hosting bill, or just loses interest. The Internet Archive's Wayback Machine, which hosts snapshots of web pages throughout their history, holds a few pieces of the puzzle, and fragments of the original lists survive in third- or fourth-hand form, in niche forums for guitarists and sports fans that haven't been updated in ten years. The whole picture is still incomplete, though. That's why the everlastingness of the PDF format is such a blessing for internet preservationists.

Whether or not Patrick Higgins consciously thought of himself as an archivist, his PDF still serves as an archive — of an era, of a digital place. Stumbling across the PDF on an Australian music school's website is a bit like finding a manuscript of Sylvia Plath's lost second novel taped underneath the sink of an interstate truck stop restroom. Or maybe more like finding Sylvia Plath's grocery shopping lists. How did it get there? Who knows! The King Kongz School of Music did not return a request for comment.

Most of the band names on this list are not serious. It was not a serious age. At one of the last possible moments when a four-person guitar-based band could hope to have any commercial or cultural viability, most of these names are studiously non-commercial, whether because they're too obscene to be named in the *Times*, or just because they're too stupid to sell to the broader public, or even to the browsers of the CD discount bin. But isn't the greatest rock band of all time named for a goofy pun about insects? Misdirection and confrontation is part of the game. My friend Mickey once had an idea for a punk band called Live Nude Oil Wrestling, just so people would see the name on the marquee of a dive bar, go in expecting one thing, and be assaulted by something else entirely. Dozens of these names operate on the same principle: Bikers Drink Free, Howie Mandel Live, Open Bar, Open Daily for Breakfast, Award-Winning Chili, Alumni Dinner, Vacation Bible School, Take Out Or Eat In, Bake Sale Next Thursday, Everything Must Go. This is to say nothing of Free Lunch, Free Parking, Free Concert, and the ever-popular Free Beer. Each name is a little one-act play about *(choose one)* bikers / breakfast lovers / cheapskates / Howie Mandel fans reading a sign outside of a dive bar, walking in, facing instant disappointment, and *(choose one)* starting a riot / complaining to the management / weeping / fleeing with their ears covered.

The list also serves as a time capsule of '90s mass culture, with allusions to Dennis Rodman, Hillary Clinton, Better Than Ezra, *The X-Files, The Bridges of Madison County*, Princess Diana, the Oklahoma City bombing, the Waco siege, Windows 95, and Hootie and the Blowfish. There are jokes borrowed from *The State, MST3K, Kids in the Hall* and *The Simpsons,* and time-capsule references to features of the Web-era digital landscape: Band.com, Duke of URL, Doubleyou Doubleyou Doubleyou. Slacker culture's obsession with syndicated daytime television comes through in names like The Philbins, The Wapners, The Original Darrens, and Kill Ted Knight. A few names are so brilliantly stupid that I still chuckle every time I read them: Shitty Shitty Band Band, Widows 95, Finger-Lickin' God, Los Netanyahus, Three Men and Another Man, The Kind of People Who Would Drink An Entire Bottle of Shampoo for $50, The Unholy Band from the Holy Land. At least a few dozen — among them, Algebra 2, Salesmen of a Divine Nature, Hurricane Megan, The New Revisionists, Crop Circles and the Circleologists Who Study Them, Pangaean Senate, 50 Gods And A Woman, Disperse Ye Rebels, Today's My Super Spaceout Day, Yours In Christ, Captain Crunch and the Let's Do Lunch — are truly just straight-up *great names for bands.*

And let's not forget Paratroopers for Jesus, of course. It's still not been claimed by a group of guitar-wielding smartasses. It was my own memory of that name that brought me to this list, fifteen years later. And now, at least, it's the name of this book.

A note on methodology and illustrations

Though perhaps 90% of the names in this book come from the Patrick Higgins / King Kongz PDF, I also accessed a handful of other band naming websites via the Wayback Machine, and added the best from three of them. The King Kongz list as originally published didn't differentiate between active bands ("This band has a great name") and hypothetical bands ("This would be a great name for a band"). After alphabetizing, reformatting and deduplicating the list, I then did my best to remove the few hundred existing bands in there. Nearly all of them came from a site called Canonical List of Weird Band Names ("these are names of actual bands"), created by an Earthlink user named Chellec, dating to the mid-1990s. Many real band names were easy to spot, like Butthole Surfers, Me First and the Gimmes Gimmes, Meat Puppets, and The Brian Jonestown Massacre. When unsure, I checked the obsessively maintained online record collector database Discogs for any trace of them. A few of the "actual band" names seemed only to exist on Chellec's list and nowhere else, so in those cases, I opted to keep them in. If Mr. Holland's Anus and Ma Joad and the Load Blowers were in fact out there playing shows and selling tapes, I apologize to their members and fans. It broke my heart to have to remove The Fearless Iranians from Hell, New Wet Kojak, Vampire State Building, Global Disrobal, The Very Idea of Fucking Hitler, and Johnny Japes and His Jesticles from this book, but so it goes. Johnny Japes and His Jesticles, if you were wondering, was a side project of Andy Partridge of XTC and English eccentric John Otway.

On the other hand, if a name was verifiably used at some point but was not particularly distinctive, I left it in: Discogs records at least five bands that have used the name Free Beer over the years, and those are just the Free Beers who got albums out. I'm sure there have been dozens more Free Beers that made it onstage at least once, and probably hundreds more Free Beers who never got out of the basement or garage.

If I could determine that a band with a name on this list didn't form until the 2000s, I left it in. After all, they may have gotten their name from one of these websites. That's the ultimate tribute you can pay to this list. Even if you choose Juicebox.

After the first edition of this book went to press, I received an email from Jason Dietz, a former USC law student now living in Portland, Oregon. He recognized many of the names on the list as coming from a site he ran in the 1990s when in law school, originally on a University of Southern California server, and later at Metacritic, the still-active review aggregation site he co-founded in 1999. The USC list is long gone, but the Metacritic list can still be accessed via the Wayback Machine. That list, in retrospect, is almost certainly the same one I remember looking at in 199-whenever, since it contained (yep!) Paratroopers for Jesus. "I would estimate that about 50-60% of the names on my list came from me," Dietz wrote via email, "with the balance from friends (and, apparently, as I check that list of names, an ex-girlfriend) and random contributors via email. How strange to think that it used to be perfectly OK to just show your personal email address online."

The illustrations that accompany each alphabetical section heading are sourced from printed clip art collections published by Dover Publications in the 1980s, mostly illustrated by artist Tom Tierney (1928-2014). These illustrations may be best remembered today as the source material for David Rees' *Get Your War On*, the much-loved satirical cartoon strip that ran from 2001-09. Though Rees' strip was a product of the post-9/11 era, the deadpan affect of '80s clip art was a prominent feature of '90s visual culture. (I remember encountering Tierney's *Office and Business Illustrations* at that art supply store I worked at in 1999, sold alongside the Das Pronto and bone folders, and being smitten. I'm sure Rees had a similar reaction.) These clip art images, which were heavily used by '90s-era zinesters, show-flier designers and graphic artists, seemed like the closest visual equivalent to the low-cost, absurdist, irony-drenched quality that these band names embody. The drier on page 31 is, I am pretty certain, the companion of the washing machine on the cover of the 1995 Sonic Youth album of that name.

Fearless Iranians From Hell, circa 1990; Vampire State Building, circa 1994.

Source: Discogs.com

0-9

$500 Reward
1-900-Botulism
10,000 Nymphomaniacs
10% Literacy Rate
1,000 Monkeys
12-Year Pedestrian
The 12-Step Program
122 Stab Wounds
13th Floor Refibulators
15 Minutes
16 Oz. Size
180 Poof
2% Lowfat
2000 Flushes
The 2x4's
30 Helens Agree
30th Century Chautauqua
3-Legged Puppy
3rd Grade Ant Farm
4 Bad Dogs
4 Cows
4 Guys Named Doris
4 Shades Blue
4 Triplets
404 Not Found
5 Lines
5 Man Band On The Head
50 Gods And A Woman
56 Middle-Sized Women
69 Days 'Til Christmas
6s And 7s
7 Acres
7 Layer Dip
7 Head Scream
7 Hours Of Blackberry Boredom
73 Large Women
9 Foot
9 Giant Pinkies
9 Invisible Ninjas Of The 99th Fuck You
90-Day Warranty
98 Little Women

A

A Better Tomorrow
A Blind Dog Stares
A Blinding Supernova Of Damning Evidence
A Box Of Fish With Tartar Sauce
A Boy Named Gomer
A Cat Born In An Oven Isn't A Cake
A Draught Of Courage
A Is For A
A Likely Story
A Little Ribbing
A Million Stupid Ways To Die
A Most Excellent Flying Death
A Nation Of Scriveners
A Pathetic Attempt At Iced Coffee
A Private Madness

A Spectacle As No Other
A Total Of Five Minutes
Aardvark Ellipse
Abatticus
The ABC Sunday Night Movie
The Abbey Normals
Ability Transplant
Able-Bodied Mayor
The Abominable Yes Men
Above Average Weight Band
Absent From Keyboard
Absolutely Flattened
Absolutely Zero
Abusive Lukes
Accidental Goat Sodomy
Accomplice
Accountants Of Death
The Accuracies
The Accusations
Ace And The Hand
Achilles Heel
Acid Popsicle
Acid Tongues
Acillatem
Acoustic Eel
Acoustic Weigh Station
Acquired Taste
Acquittal
Action Max And The Packages
Action Painting
Actual Size
Acute Health Risk
Ad Wizards
Adam's Rib House
Addendum
Addicted To Amputation
The Additives
Addressee Unknown

The Adherents
Admiral Bartholomew Hawthorne's All Nude Revue
Admiral Poopy Pants And His Dancing Teeth
Adult Burgers
The Adult Caretakers
Adult Content
Adult Diaper
Advancing Army
The Adventures
Adventures In Shrubbery
Adversary
The Advil Monkeys
The Aef
Aeolian Hasp
Aesop Was A Zebra
Affordable Floors
Afghanistan Banana Stand
African Legends
After Bingo
Afterdinner Mint
The Afternoon Biafrans
Aftershock
Afterthought
Age Of Raisin
Ages Of Yellow
Aggressive Crotch Display
Agnes Morehead
The Agnews
Ah-Choo
Air Beeters
Air Businessman
Air Force One
Air-Conditioned Pie
The Airbags
Airedale Chowder
Airport Smut
Alas

Alfred Is Leaving
Algebra 2
Alice on Brains
Alien Nymphos From Uranus
Alien Response Team
Alive Alive O
All At Once
All For Nothing
All That Glitters
All Thumbs
All You Can Eat
Alligator Control
Alliteration State
Almost Forever
Alomar Spit
Alphabet Soup
Already Ready Already
Altered Ego
Altered Logic
Altered Sensation
Altered Spatio-Temporal Perception
Alternate Monkey Disposal Unit
Alternate Route B
The Alternates
Aluminum Breakfast
Alumni Dinner
Always A Hoax
Always Robert
AM/FM
Amanda's Dreaming
The Amateurs
The Amazing Life And Times Of Warren G. Harding
Ambidextrous Motorist
Ambrosia Salt Pie
Amen To That
America U.K.
America's Sweetheart
American Day
The Amish
Amorpha
An Idea Destroying Itself Through Perception
An Offer You Can't Refuse
Anaclotomy
Anal Banal
Anal Beard Barbers
Anal Bingo
Anal Canal
Anal Geriatrics
Anal Vortex
Analog Abacus
The Analyticals
And Many More
And Your Little Dog
The Andes
Anemic Intensity
Angel Mummies
Angel Of Cleveland
Angel's Egg
Angelfish Food
Angelic Cemetery
Angels' Fear Cake
Angle Of Attack
Angled Saxophone
Angry Burrito
Angry Commuters
Angst In Space
Anhedonia
Animal Electro-Magnetism
Animal Farm
Annie's Savior
Annual Report
Anomalous Reading
Anomie
Anomoly
Anonymity

Anonymouse
Ant Pants
Ant Tracks
Anticrust
Antimatter
Antique Rockers
Anybody's Guess
Anything But Water
ANZAC
Apocalypso!
Apogee
Apoca Lips
Apple Brown Betty And The Blintz Victims
Apple Killers
Apprehension Monitor
Aqua Vulva
Aquajoy
Aquatic Donuts
The Aquiline Expressions
Archaeological Dig
Archaeopteryx
Archaic Bulb
The Arbitrary Placement Of Walls
Archers In Tweeds
Architecture Of Neglect
Arctic Circle Jerks
Are These My Pants?
Are You Crazy?
Are You Okay?
Are You Seated Comfortably
Area Rugs
Arena Football
The Arisen
Arizona Desert
Arizona Tongue
Armed Robbery
Armpit Of The Central One
Armpit Tarts
Arms And Legs Akimbo
Army Brat
Army Of Lawyers
Army Of Prawns
Arooogah!
Art House
The Artificial Inseminators
Artificial Lamb
Artificial Light
Artificial Street Smarts
Art Traitor
The Artist Currently Known As Prince
Arts And Leisure Section
Aryan Superqueer
As My Skin Keeps Shrinking
As You Read This So Shall You Be Damned
ASCII Music
Ashtray Man
Aspects Of Culture
Asphalt
Ass Solutions, Inc.
Assault And Battery
Assault Rifle Sale
Asserted Urge
The Assessors
Assorted Sizes
Asthma Sheep
Astral Crapshoot
Asynchronous Transfer Mode
At Every Turn
At The Top Of The List
At War
At Wit's End
Atom Gong
Atomic Aardvark From Pasadena
Atomic Circuit

Atomic Clunk
Atomic Mushroom
Atomic Ted And The
  Heinous Boys
Atomic Wait
The Attack Of The Green
  Slime Beast
The Attempts
Attn: Deficit Disorder
Auction Block
The Auditors
Augmentation
Aunt Betty Is Crying
Aunt Edna
Aunt Spiker
Australians Live
  Upside-Down
Authorized Personnel
Autoerotic Nightmare
Automatic Monotone
Automaton
Autumn Ash
Aversion Bride
Averted Eyes
Avocado Riot
Aw Heck
Aw.
Award-Winning Chili
Axis And Allies

B

B-Bye
Baader Loves Meinhoff
Baal
Babes Ahoy
Babes In Boyland
Babushka Lady
Baby Makes Three
Baby Shit Brown
Back Seat Drivers
Back To Work
Bacon And Eggs
Bad Chocolate
Bad Haircuts
Bad Influence
Bad Neighbours With Good
  Gardens
Badical Turbo Radness
The Badushkas
Bag Bag
Bag Of Chow
Baggy Elbow Skin
Bagpipe Hendrix
Bake Sale Next Thursday
Baked Not Fried
Bakin' Brownies
Baking Soda Toilet Paper
The Bald Shatners
Bale Wolves Of The Greater
  Howling Dark
Ball Night
Ballistic Quickies
Baltimore Aureoles
Banana Barbeque
Banana Flash
Banana Hammock
Bananas In Heat
Band In A Box

Band Of Scoundrels
Band Of The Century
Band Of The Lost
Band On A Stick
Band o' Coots
Band.com
Banana Dan And The Bandanas
Bandini Mountain
Bandnamed Out
BandNet
Bandyleg
Bang A Ueey
Bank Ahoy
Bankers Selling Moonbeams
The Baptoids
Barbara, A Rabbi
Barber Code
Barbicide
Barbie Pudding
The Barbs
Barely Manilow
Bargle
Baritone Brisk
The Barneys
Barnyard Ballers
Barnyard Sleestack
The Barrage
Barrel O' Monkeys
Barren Lifeless Rock
The Barristers
Barry Cleanser
Baseball Oscillate Nylon Hug
Based In Theory
Basement Tapes
Bashin' Budgies
Basic-Basic
The Basics
The Basic Necessities

The Basketball Emperors Of The Milky Way Galaxy
Basketcaps
Bastion
Bat Crinkle
Bathroom Tourism
Bathtub Holiday
The Baton Of Jingoism
Battle Breasts
Battle Of The Network Stars
Bauxite Ores
Bayonet Swim
Be Nice
The Be-Dulls
Beach Toy Lentils
The Beaks
Beanpole Lookalikes
Bearded Clambake
Bearer Of Indifferent Tidings
The Bearskin Boys
Beat Stompers
Beat Up The Easter Bunny
The Beatlers
Beatles U.S.
The Beatlets
Beats Me
Beautiful Gate
Beautiful Remark
Beautiful Solvent
Beauty Contest
Because We're Penguins
Bedpan Drinkers
Beef Stew And The Monster Trucks
Beef Silhouette
Beefcake Development
The Beerbrains
Before And After
Behind In The Count
Behind The Curtain

Belkin Data Switch
Ben Hur And Beth Him
The Bends
The Benny Hinn Fan Club
Bent Fred
Bernie The Trailer Park
Bertha Makes Landfall
Bertrand Clay
Best Before August 12
Best Behaviour
Bestial Sandwich
Beta Boy
Beta Male
Better Than Mustaf
Better Than Nehemiah
Better Than Pearl Jam
Betti Yeti
Betty Ford Clinic
Betty's Fish Bag
Between Life And Death
Between One And Ten
Beware Of God
Bevy Of Incompetents
Beyond All Reason
Beyond Recognition
Bhoy Dies Young
The Bibs
Biding Time
The Biffs
Biff And Muffy
Big Al's Gas House
Big Ass Truck
Big Being
Big Black Monolith
Big Chum
Big Circumstance
Big Coke
Big Daddy Cumbuckets
Big Deal
Big Dropoff

Big Dirt Nap
The Big Eighth Grader
The Big Foam
Big Government
Big Hazel
Big Grumble
Big Hairy Euglena
Big Hairy Wart
Big Hand Full
Big Hand On The One
Big Help
Big Improvement
Big Insect In The Cecum
Big Negatory
Big Ole Thang
The Big One
Big Plastic Head
The Big Problem
Big Purple Marker
Big Sandwich
Big Save
Big Screen Nude Explosions
Big Silly
Big Splits
Big Tex
Big Thoughts for Small
   Heads
Big Whoop
Bigger
Bigger Than A Bread Box
The Biggest Names
   In Show Business
Biggie Angioplasty
The Biggies
Bigmouth Bass
Bikers Drink Free!
Bikini Area Code
Bikini Atoll
Bikini Model
Bikini Oil

The Bile
Bill And His Mother
Billary Clinton's Pet Donkey
Billy, Take Your Ritalin
Bing And The Cherries
Binomial Nomenclature
Bio Bag
Biocontrol Road
Bird Loaf
Bird Of Paradise
Biscuit
Bismarck's Noble Mustache
Bitch Magnet
Bitch Transmission
The Bitches Of Madison County
Bite Marks
Biting Thyme
Bitter Business Bureau
Bizarre Gardening Accident
Bjeck
Black Border
Black Crackers
Black Pearl Angel
Black Powder Biscuit
Black Wednesday
Bladder In A Can
Bland Acrimony
Bland Leonardo
Blark
Bleeding The Fifth
The Bleeding Toothpicks
Blend Dream
Blender Babies
Blew Willie
Blind Flyer
The Blinkers
Blip
The Bliss Bandits
Blix
The Blizzard Tickets
Bloat
Bloaters Ball
The Bloated Tires
Blog
Blond Mongolia
Blondy Brunette
Blood And Gore
Blood Sport
Blood Sundae
Bloodmobile
The Bloody Gloves
Bloody Machine Of Fright
Bloody Stools
Blot
Blow It Up
Blow Job Queen
Blow The Man Down
Blown Gasket Boys
Blown To Bits
Bludgeon
Bludgeonfist
Blue Bottle
Blue Boy Suffocation Syndrome
Blue Collar Suzie
Blue Disease
Blue Foods
Blue Funk
The Blue Genes
Blue Grassholes
Blue In The Face
Blue Jean Junkies
Blue Pointer
Blue Ring Octopus
Blue Shark
Blue Ska
Blue Tongue
Blue Vein
Blue Water

Blue-Bellied Black Snake
Blueberry Werewolf
Bluebottle
The Blunders
The Blunt Objects
Blunt Trauma
Blurt
Bob's Magic Flea Circus
Boba Frett
Bobbing For Heart Attacks
Bobby-Dazzler
Body Cavity
Body Slam!
The Bog People
Bogus Men In An Upside Down Boat
Boiled Pig
Bomb Pop
Bomb Seattle
Bon Jovi's Witnesses
Bone Dough
Bonehead One-Liners
Bongo Mist
Bong Resin Bocce Balls
Bonzo Madrid
Boobadatuba
Boom Squad
Boomerang
The Bootleggers
The Booty Conspiracy
Border Patrol
Borderline Stupid
The Bores
Boris And The Bucketsuds
Bork Bork Bork
Born Screaming
Born This Way
Born To Die
Bosco's Sheep-Playing Orchestra
The Bosporus
Bottom Dollar
The Bottom Dwellers
Bottoms Up
Bounce Around
The Bovines
Bowling Alarm
Bowling Ball On A Swivel
Bowling Shoes
Box Car Bimbo
Box For It
Boxing Cats
Boy Meets Grill
Boy Meets Squirrel
The Boy Who Cried Your Mom
Boycott
The Boys
Bra Strap Pluckers
The Brackets
Brad And Janet
Brain Jelly
Brainpan Alley
The Brave 600
Breakfast Barrel
Breakfast Tables
The Breakup Boys
The Breakups
The Breechloaders
Bridal Shower Nuclear Tragedy
Bridgehead
The Bridges Of Madison Avenue
The Brie Nibblers
Brigadoons
Bright Idea
Bright New Death
Bright Vision
Brillo Facecloth

Bring A Lawyer
Bring Me A Radish
Broken Fifth
The Bronchial Tubes
Bronze Age
Broom Hockey
Brown Paper Babies
Brown Spider
Brown Star Pudding
Bruised Tailbone
Brumby
Brunhilde
Bub Slug's Lottery Ticket
Bubble Gumshoe
Bubbleator
Bucket O'Brine And His Travelling One-Man Band
Bucket Full Of Heresy
Bucket Squad
Buckshot Plumage
Buddy Funk
Budooshka
Buffalo Yogurt
Buffer Zone
Bug Grumble
Bug Spray
The Bug Zapper Of Desire
Buggy Wreck
Bulk Bins
Bullet Brush
Bullet Joe
Bullet Pulley
Bulletproof Pope
Bum Juice
Bum Rap
Bumper Car
Bundt Cake Fiasco
The Bundts
Bungalow Attic
Bunk Pand
Bunny Foot Charm
Burger Pimp
Buried Treasure
Burn Factory
Burn Unit
Burn Your Tongue
Burning Britches
Burning Lesbians
Burning Pedestrian
Burning Smell
Burnt Toast And Oranges
Burning Waterbeds
Burnt To A Cinder
Burt And Alien Burt
Bus #5
Business Reply Mail
Buster Dude
Buster G. And The Family
Buster Hose
The Bustles
But Soft
Butt Chili
The Butt Nuggets Of Joy
Butt Savages
Butt Squeegee
Buttafuoco And Menendez
Butterloaf
Butternuts
Butthole Macrame
Buttsex Smurf
Buttsteak
Buy This Harp
Buzzclip
By A Landslide
By A Wire
By Jingo
By The Book
The By-Laws
Bye-Bye Juice
The Byzanteens

C

Cab Forward
Cabbage Apple Dustbin
Cabin Fever
The Cads
Caffeine Confusion
Caffeine Psychosis
Cain't Spel Nuthin'
Cairo Under Newer Texas
The Cake
Calamari
Calculated Slide
Calculus Class
The Call
Call Security
Call The Cops
Call Waiting
Calling All Cars
Calling Card
Camouflage Tattoo
Can Do
Can I See It?
Can You Say Ruddfucker's?
Can't Spell Albuquerque
The Canadian System
Canary Eyelids
Cancer Bunny
Candy Filter Tip
Candy For Cats
Candy Punks
Candyman Messiah
The Canisters
Canned Monster
Canned Sock Sweat
Canopy
Cantankerous Ankylosaur
Cantaloupe Commons
Cantilever Maybe
The Cap Masters
Cap-M
Capital Idea
The Captain And Schlemiel
Captain Crunch And The Let's Do Lunch
Captain Drinking Binge
Captain Hook And The Impotent Seamen
Captain Infinity And The Standard Deviation
Captain Obvious
Captain Spaulding
Captain Wildlife And The Carbon Copy
Car Sickness
Carbonated Chicken Feathers
Carbonation
Cardboard Loner
Cardinal Ankles
Cardinal Sin
The Cardsharks
Careful
Careless Perfectionists
Carlito And The Electrical Spaniards
Carnivorous Sal
Carp Hemisphere
Carrot-Strewn Paradise
Cartesian Rationalism

Case Study
Cash Money
Cash On Hand
Caspar The Holy Ghost
Castor Oil
Casual Day
Casual Tweeds
The Casualties
Cat Have Pancreas
Cat Head
Catalog Sales
Catastrophic Failure
Caterpillar Grows Up
Catface Would Like To Have A Ham Sandwich Please
Cathedral Of Lunch
Cats In A Blender
Cats On Heat
Cattle Dust
Cattlist
Caught With Our Pants Down
Caustic Oboe
Cavalcade Of Tripe
Cave Canem
Cease And Desist
Celebrity Glass Eye Anal Beads
Celebrity Rump Roast
Celery Head
Celestial Toymaker
Cellophane
Cement Fajita
The Centaurs
Cerebral Erection
Certain Death
Certainly Sir
Chad And The Sudan
Chainsaw Ninjas
The Chair
Champions Of the New West
Championship Knickers
Chancre
Change Of Pace
Change Of Venue
Channel 80
Channels Of Distribution
The Chaotics
Chaplain Stick
Character Generator
Charibdis
Charisma Factor
Charity Stripe
Charlie Hustle
Charlie The Amazing Chronic Foot
The Charo Chronicles
Charon's Special
Cheap Retreat
Cheap Toy Roundup
Cheapo Depot
Check, Please
Checkerboard
Cheeky Pelican
Cheese Factor
The Cheeseburgers From The Black Lagoon
Cheeses Of Nazareth
Chef Nielsen And His Crew
Chef's Pyjamas
Cher UK
Cherry Coke Enema
Chew The Dog
Chewbacca Plaid Cock
Chewing Cud
Chewing On A Gambit
Chia Slut
Chicago Will Be Ours
Chick Magnet
Chickadee Spin
Chicken Fish
Chicken George

Chicken Obituary
Chickens On X
Chickup
Child Stars
Childbirth Shot-Put
Childproof Capone
Children Of The Love Machine
Children Of The Vending Machine
Chilean Links
Chill, Baby
Chimps With Hammers
Chinchilla Rest Stop
Chinese Egg Catalog
Chintz Tinsel
Chipped Figurine
Chirpes
Chit-Chat
Chock
Chocolate Eyeball Junction
Cholesterol Is My Lex Luthor
Chomp
Chopped Lips And The Pincers
Chortle
Christ On A Crutch
Christ On A Stick
Chronic Halogen Toast
The Chubbies
The Chumps
The Chunkers
The Chunks
The Church Of Cod
The Churners
Churning
Cinnamon Canine
Circuit
Circumference
Circumstance
The Citizens
Citizens Of The Cretaceous
Citrus
Civil Code
Clam
Clammy Cerements
Clarence Is In My Shower
Class Clown
Classical Trash
Clatter
Claxon
Clean Dog City
Clean Underpants
Clean Your Guilotine
Cleanup Crew
Clear Fog
Clearly Labeled Rodent
Cliche
Click
Click Here To Continue
Click Him, Too
Cliff And The Notes
Climbing Air
The Clinical Dead
Clinton's Sex Diary
Clog
Close To Arnold
Closed
Closed Until Further Notice
The Closet Monkeys
The Cloven Hooved
Clown Cheese
The Clowns
Clue
Clue Grenade
Clunk
Clunky
Clusterfunk
The Coaches Association
Coalition 349
Cob
Cobain's Brains

Cobalt Malt
Cobalt Salted Device
Coccyx
Cockeyed Suzie
Cocktail Party
Cockroach Cookbook
Coconut Lightbulb
The Coelacanths
Coffee Achievers
Coffee Ground Emeritus
Cold Speculum
Cold Squiggle
Cold War
Cole Slaw Buffet
Cole Slaw Generation
Colon Pow!
Colossus
Colosteamer
Combustible Frogling
Come Back In Five Minutes
Come Here Rotunda
Come In, Please
Comes In A Cup
Comes Up Swinging
Coming Back From France
Coming To Blows
Commercial Interruption
Commie Red Bastards
The Commission
Commissioner
Commodity Fetish
Common Trap
Communal Mayonnaise
Communist Iced Tea
Communist Synthesizers
Compact Lunch
Complete Fiasco
Complete Set
Compost Boy
Compound Fracture
Compromising Engineers

Compulsive Liars
Concrete Bashful Girl
Concrete Mind
Concrete Squatters
The Condemned
The Condoms
Conehead Immolation
Conflict Of Interest
Congratulations
The Connivers
The Consequences
Consequences In Marinara Sauce
Considerable Jesus
Conspiracy Of Peace
Constant Pain
Constipated Goats
Consumer Confusion
Contemporary Hit Radio
Content Providers
Continents
Continuity Problem
Continuum
Contract
Control Group
Contusion Soup
The Convenient Locations
The Conversationalists
Conveniently
Cooking With Heat
The Cookware Set
Cool Million
The Coolest Thing
Cooling-Off Period
The Coordinators
Coors Chorus For Lunch Bunch
Copernicus Loaf
Coprolite
Coprolite Dip
The Coprolites

Coprophage
Copyright Infringement
Corder Roy
Corn Chutney
Corn Cob Data
Corn Job
Corporal Klinger
Corporate Greed
Corpse Circus
Corpsus De Nautae
Corpus Christi
Corrugated Cows
Corrupted Endeavour
Corsican Hair
Cortex Blowout
Cosmic Coal
Cosmic Corruption
Cosmodrome
The Cost Reduced Band
Cotopaxi
Could Be Worse
Counterattack
Counting Sheryl Crows
Country Slaughter
The Course Of Evolution
Cousin Eddie
Cover Story
Cow Cuds
Cowboy Proctors From Akron
Cowboy Warehouse
Crab Nebula
Cracked Jug
Crackle
Craft Work
Cranium
Cranky Pants
Cranky Plumber
Crap Car
Crash Positions
The Craters
Crawfish Boat Shirt
Crayon Logic
Crazy Evelyn
Crazy For Bovines
Crazy Peace
Crazy Taco Cafeteria
Crazymaker
Cream Lemon
Creamy Cubic Zirconia Centers
Cream Rinse
The Creation Of The Universe Was A Beautiful Thing
The Creationists
Creative License
Creator
Creature Features
The Credentials
Creeping Phlox
Crewsay Ouyay
Crime Lab
Criminal Attitude
Crimper Joe And The Flying Buffoons
Crippling Orgasms
Crisis Prevention Network
Crisp Pig Fritters
Crispity Crunchity
Crispy Nostrils
C.R.I.T.I.C.
Critical List
Crook Depository
Crop Circles And The Circleologists Who Study Them
Cross-Cultural Sex-Role Crises
Cross-Platform Launch

Crossover Appeal
The Croutons
Crucifix Child
The Crude Ale Ensemble
Crunchy Granola
Crunchy Astrolabe
Cry 909
Cry Rusty Clock
Cry Stupid Chimp
Crybaby Skater
Cryptic Crisp
Crystal Blue Eurasian
Crystal Powder
Cubix Rube
Cuisine
Cult Of One
Cultural Alzheimers
Cure For Cancer
Curfew
The Curiosities
The Currency Of Spain Is The Potato
The Current Addressees
Current Events
Curriculum Vitae
The Curs
Customer Service
Cut It Out
Cutting Down My Friend's Oak
Cutting Edge Music
Cyanide
Cyberbuggy
Cybermimer
Cybernixon
Cyborgnine
Cyclonic Cooking
The Cyclopes
The Cygnets
Cyrillic Characters

D

Da Rok Sox
Dad And The Mothers
Daddy Goes To Jail
Daddy Hangups
Daddy Said So
Daffy's Resume
Dagger
The Dailies
The Dainty Mincers
The Dairyaires
Daisy Fart
Dale Juice
Dali's Movement Disorder
Dammit
Damn All Goodness
Damned If You Do
Dan Of Poughskeepsie
The Dana Mulders
The Dana Plato Gang
Dances With Women
Dancing In Sarajevo
Dandruff
Danger, Falling Rocks
Dangerous Curve
Dangerous Pastries
The Dangers Of Organized Dancing
Dangle
The Danglers
Dangling Ganglia

Dante's Followers
Dark Gloaming
Dark Influence
Dark Light
Dark Velvet
Darn It
Data Capture
Dating The Tooth Fairy
David Lee Oswald Harvey Roth
A Day In The Life Of Death
Day Of European Oppression
Day Rager
Dead At The Wheel
Dead Bird
The Dead Bodyguards Of Abraham Lincoln
Dead Budd
Dead Cat
Dead Cat Bounce
The Dead Clintons
Dead Dog
Dead Immortals
Dead People
The Deadly Mums
Deadworld
Dearly Beloved
Death By Elocution
Death Incarnate
Death Pickle
Death Pony
Death Warmed Over
Debarcation Procedure
Debt Toupee
Decade Of Failure
Decayed Recognizer
Decaying Infrastructure
Deceased Communists
Deciduous
Deconstructive Surgery
The Deeds
Deep Feeling
Deep Space 90210
Deer In The Headlights
Deficit Reduction
Definite Scrawl
The Deflectors
The Defunct
Delay Of Game
Delayed Reaction
The Delegations
Delicate Flaky Crust
Demon Woe And The Fifty Cows And The Thirty Pigs And The Twenty Chickens
Dental Records
Dental Threat
Dental Torture
Department Manager
Departmental Regulations
Depleted Resources
Depression Chamber
Der Sippe Gott
Derby Night
The Derelict Aunties
The Derisions
Derived By Indecision
Describe Yourself In Two Words Or Less
Desert Forest
Deserted Island
Designated Drinkers
Deskjet 540
Desperate Inspiration
Dessert Topping
Destination Saturn
Destruct Sequence
Destruction Clause
Detonator

Devastation Direct
The Devil You Don't
Dewey And The Decimal System
The Deweys
Dialysis
Diane's Tic
Diarrhetics
Dick Hertz
Dictator Shift
Die And Let Live
Die Crapula Die
Diecast Messiah
Diet Of Worms
Diet Plan
Diet Smoke
Different Drummer
Digital/Analog Crisis
Digital Toque
Dihydrogen Monoxide
Dilated Orifice
Diles Mavis
DiMaggio's Triumph
Dime A Dozen
Dime Authority
Dimmer Switch
The Dingleberries
The Dingy Ginghams
Dinky Howser
Diorama Night
Dinner on Me
Diocese Delight
Diode
The Diplomatics
Dipsmiths
Diphthong
Diphthong Dilly
Direct Hit
Dirk Pitty
Dirt Creme
Disc Rib
Discarded Sausage Casings
Discernably Turgid
The Dirty Looks
Dirty Movies
Dirty Spider
Disabled List
Disappointing Ball
Disaster Planning
The Disclaimers
Disco And Dot Matrix
Discorporate People Drinking Beer
Discover Pluto
Discussion Group
Disembodied Tiki Head
The Dishes
Dishonorable Discharge
Dismemberment Clause
Disperse Ye Rebels
Disposable Thumbs
Distant Star
Distemper
Divine Wind
The Divorce Lawyers
Dizengoff Bomb Squad
DJ Doo Doo
DJ Jazzy Yeltsin
DNA Test
Do I Get My Box Of Steaks?
Do I Look Fat
Do You Smell Dad?
Dodgy Curry
Dog Fox Gone To Ground
Dog Lipstick
Dog Molar
Dog Skills 101
The Dog Totem
Dog Will Hunt
The Doges

Dogmatic Johnson
Dollar Lane
Dollar Pints
Dolly Grip And The Best Boys
The Don Schlong Trio
Don The Mask
Don't Ask Me, I'm Not Here
Don't Bite The Sun
Don't Call Me Skaface
Don't Do That
Don't Fucking Dare
Don't Tell
Don't Try This At Home
Donald Sutherland's Butt
Donkeymaker
Donner Party Leftovers
Donut Blond
Donut Gall
Doo Dah Day
Doom And Discrepancy
Doom In A Room
The Doomed
Doomsday Machine
Dope Shafty And The Syringes
The Dopes
Dopey Bear
Doppler Affect
The Dorks
Dorsal Turette
Dos Grandes Pechos
Dot Matrix And The Plotters
Double Coupons
Double Digits
Double Helix
Double Negative
Double Overtime
Double Secret Probation
Double Time
Doubleyou Doubleyou Doubleyou
Down In Flames
Down Pat
Down Time
Downchuck
Dowry 007
Dr. Al Kemmey And The Colossus Of Rhodes
Dr. Humenansky And The Recovered Memories Of Abuse
Dr. Mauve And The Quezzy Dream
Dr. Overdub
Dr. Pornograffitti
Dr. Sphincter
Dr. Zeus
Dr. Zoffiss
Drag Queen Barbie
Dragon Slayers
Drained Cows
Drambuie Drosophiliac
The Drastically Reduced
Draw A Goat
Drawing Blanks
The Drawn And Quartered
Dream As Henry
Dream Flight
Dream Ticket
Dreamcycle
Dregs Kill Jesus
Dress Slackers
Dress to the Left
Dressing Down
Dried Up Ol' Jim
The Drill Thralls
Drinks On The House
Drippy
Drive-Thru Religion

Drizzle Stick
The Droll
The Droplets
Drug Czars
Druggernaut
Drugzilla
Drum Of Scum
Drums Of Fu Manchu
Drunk And Sleazy
Drunken Star Wars Extras
Dry Clean Only
Dry Goods
The Dubious Distinctions
Ducal Shoes
Duck Crossing
Duck Feet
Duck!
Dude Stuff
Dueling Harpsichords
Duff Paddie
Duke Of URL
Dum Tee Dum
Dumbassachistic Love Child
Dumber Than A...
Dunk Tank
Duodenum Bight
The Duplications
The Dust Busters
Dust Cake
Dusty Lust
Dwarves Crying Giant Tears
Dwellers Of The Necropolis
The Dying Gauls
Dynamo Hum
Dynasty Of Planet Chromada
Dysfunction Complex
Dysgenesis
Dyson Sphere
Dyspeptic!

E

E-Mail Sid And The Hard Drive
E-Meter
E-Ticket Ride
Ear Off
Earl Lester And The Foggy River Mountain Valley Boys
Earthlings On Fire
Earwax
East Of Midnight
Easy To Serve
Eat My Taxes
Ebert In Shorts
Ecclesiastical
Echelon Blue
Echo Layer
Ecology Dick
The Economy
Ed's Redeeming Qualities
Eden Bound
Eden Spurned
Eels In The Sink
Eeyore Ass Guzzlers
Egg Parade
Egg Roll Wipe
Egregious Spum
Either/Either
El Grupo Sexo
The El-Rons
Elaborate Hoax
Elastic Fudge A-Go-Go

Elastic Mag And The Weighty Problem
Elastic Sausage
Electric Codpiece
Electric Dwarf
Electric Jesus
Electric Satyr
The Electronettes
Element Of Surprise
The Elementals
Elements Of Style
The Eleventh Hour
Elk's Ass, Montana
Elucidation Zone
Elvis From The Waist Up
The Emasculator Graham
Embarrassing Flag
Embarrassing Stain
Emergency!
Emotion In Motion
Emotional Baggage
Emotional Blackmail
Emperor Xochimilco and the Champions Of Sin
Employee Of The Month
The Empty Vessel
Emu Jerky
Encephalitis Gumbo
The Encounters
Encroachment
Encumberment
The Encyclopedia Satanica
The End Of All Male Guilt
Endgame Soliloquy
Endive Squad
The Endless Abyss
Endless Placenta
English Channel 7
Enhanced For Your Exclusive Pleasure
The Enigmatics
Enis
Enlargement
Ennui Innuendo
Enormous Pull
Enough Already
Enuma Elish
Epiglottal Duplicate
Epstein-Barr Band
The Equally Attractive Non-Alcoholic Beverages
Equality Of Sleaze
Equine Supremacy
Ergonomic Intrigue
Ernest Goes To Beirut
Eros Rampant
Ersatz Glow
Escalated Risk
Escape Modulator
Escher Tennis
Esperanto Oblivion
The Establishment
Esther's Roll
Ethelred The Unready
Etheria
Ethnocentric
Eton B. Eaton
Eucalyptus
Euclid Malfunction
Euglena Delight
Evaporated Fats
Evening Constitutional
The Evening News
Evening Screamer
Event Staff
Eventual Crisis
Evergreen
Every Burnt Lozenge
Every Citizen's Greatest Fear

Everything Must Go
Everything You Read
Evil Clowns
Evil Doings
Evil Edna's Satellite Children
Evil Eye
Evil Kanevils
Evil Trousers
Evil Twin Skippy
Evil Wind
Evincing Viscera
Exchange Students
Exhuming Rasputin
Exit Poll
Exoglab
Experimental BBQ
Experimental Bear Suit
Explanatory Dictum
Expletive Deleted
Exploded Ghost
Exploding Head Trick
Exploding Macaroon
Exploitation
Exploring Sharpening Variations
Expressions And Eyebrows
Extinction by Default
Extra Fine Pilot
Extra Medium
Extra Pep
Extremely Boring
Extremely Oversensitive Poets
Extremely Tall Flowers
Extrusion Talker
Exxon Bill
Eye Of God
Eyelids Of The Future
Eyewitness News

F

F'in Hamster Rebuttal
Fab Cleaver
Fabulous Pimps
Facelift
Fascist Undergarment
Faculty X
Failed Radiation Experiment
Failing Nations
Fair Game
Fair Play For Cuba
Fair Today
Fairy Tonic
Fait Accompli
Fake Mistake
Fake Tan
Fall Colors
The Fall Of The House Of Usher
Falling Flames From The Bomb
Falling From My Friend's Oak
The F.A.L.S.E. Pretenses
False Testimony
Family Feudalists
Fan Effect
Fancy Lads
Fancy Zandal
Fantasy Eyeland

The Far And Away
Far From Gerald
Far From Luke
The Far Out Groovy
Farewell To A Cold Corpse
Farm Auction
Farm-Fresh Lemonade
Farrt
Fart Kazoo
The Fartz
Fat Chantz
Fat Cyclops
Fat Dominoes
Fat Elvis
Fat Head
Fat Rolls
Fatal Sneeze
The Fatals
Fatback
Fatherland
The Faucet Drips
The Fault Tolerant Band
Faux Amis
Fax
Fear, Uncertainty And Doubt
Fear Of Pain
Fear Of Water
Feet On A Stick
The Feints
Felcher
Felonious Punk
Felt Smart
Female Wallace
Feral Kings
The Fernmore Shootmasters
Ferntide
Fescue Platter
Festive Gaiety
Fetal Drone

Fetid World
The Fetus Eaters
Fetus Frenzy
Fetusacopia
Feverish Hymn
Ffffaaarrrrtttt
Field Trip Permission Slip
Fifi Skipped The Country With A Nazi
The Fifth Beatles
The Fight Or Flight Attendants
Figpace
Filter Cartridges
The Filth Amendment
Filthy, Filthy Donna
Filthy Lucre
Filthy Luka
Filthy Mitten
The Finals
Fine Print
The Fine Washables
Finger Fusion
Finger In The Dyke
Finger Paste Burglars
Finger Thirst
Finger-Lickin' God
Fingernail Blister Hockey
Fire At The Wall
Fireflies In The Corn
First Prize
First Quarter
Fish Like Water
Fish Lips
Fish Meets Bait
Fish Soda
Fishing With Cyril
The Fishtubes
Fission Of Irma
Fist Contract

The Fisticuffs
Five Hairy Dweebs
Five In A Maze
Five Liver Robot
Five Of A Kind
Five Potato
Five Reasons
Five Star Hotel
The Fixations
Fjord Glassblower Claims Jonquil
Flambookey
Flamin' Schnanuses
Flaming Box Of Ants
The Flaming Chainsaws
The Flaming Donuts Of Jesus
The Flange
Flanksteak Jones And The G45 Space Unit
Flargabag
Flash
Flash Pants
Flash the Badge
Flashback 500
Flat Imagination
Flat Out
Flatlino
Flatus Maximus
Flatuliners
Flavors Of Ferocity
Flea Bargain
Flemish Blemish
Flency And The Elvin Trove
Flick!
The Flickings
Flight Crew
Flight Of The Nimbus
Flime Ties
Flippant Hosiery
The Flippers
Flock Uh Hillbillies
Floppy Disc Brakes
Floppyface
Floss
Flower Child
Fluffy Carbonation
Fluid Motion
Fluorescent Wax Museum
Flux Patrol
The Flux Pavilion
Flux Ping-Pong
Fly Molo
Flying Aztecs
The Flying Mallets
Foam Booth
Fog Art Presentation
The Follow-Ups
The Follow-Ups
The Food Groups
The Foot-Longs
The Fops
For Kids
For Pete's Sake
The Force Fields
Force Vomit
Forchestra
Forced Roadkill
Forever
Forget About It
Form Of Submission
Formula For Success
Fornicators
Forty Foot Wall Of Puke
The Fossils
Fountain Drink (Large)
Four Dweebs
Four Hookers And Roy's Tiger
Four Man Bridal Shower

Four More Years
Four Peach
Four Point Restraints And A Lobster Bib
The Four Quintuplets
Fourchestra
Fourplay
The Fourth Reich
Fox Force Five
Foxx Network
Fractured Eyelash
Frank And Sense
Frank Snotra
Frankenstein Drag Queens
Frantic Symphony Of Languid Pink
Freak House
Freakiller
The Freaky Executives
Fred Pencil
Fred University
Fred's Abominable Butt-Man
Free Beer
Free Beer And Chicken
Free Concert
Free Finks
Free Hate
Free Lunch
Free Parking
Free Range Chicken
Free Wheels
Freedom
Freeze Tag
Freezer Burn
French Insult
French Roast
Frenzy
Frequent Flyers
Frequently Asked Questions
The Frescoes
Fresh And Exciting
Fresh Produce
Fresh Water
The Fresheners
Freshness Dated
Freud Cobra
The Freudian Slips
Freudian Slits
Fried Parasols
The Friendly Catheter Salesmen
The Friends Of Oatmeal
Friendly Fire
Fright Behavior Test
Frog Pound
Frog Tongue
Frogs Can Get Dead
Frolic And Detour
From Planet 13
Front Porch
Froot Moebius Loops
Frosted Horsefly
The Froth
Frozen Load
Frozen Orange
Frozen Solid
Frozen Throes
Fruit Flakes
Fruit Mover
Fuck Me I'm Irish
Fuck Me Jesus
Fuck You Yankee Bluejeans
Fuck Your Shitty Planet
Fuckin' Shit Biscuits
Fuckin' Son Of A Bitch
Fucking Angels
Fudge Puddle
Fudge Tunnel
Full Circle

Full Count
Full Editorial Control
Fullyclothed Ladies
Fumbutoid
Fuming Merrily Away
Fun For Dad
Fun House
Fun Truckin' With Jesus
Fun With The Lunchlady
Fun-Loving Barnyard
    Animals
Fungilli
Fungus
Fungus Fling
Fungus Mungus
Funky Chicken
Funky Crib Death
Funky In A Bad Way
Funny Bone
Funs 'N' Poses
Furniture God
The Furtives
The Fury
Fusion School
Fuss
Future Booth
The Future Of Work And
    Power
Future Smell Of London
Fuzzy Backside
Fuzzy Buddhists
Fuzzy Monkey

G

The G-Forces
G.I. Ants
Gack
Gadzooks
Gaffa
Galapagos Approaching
The Gall Bladders
Gall Stone Goulash
Galook
Galvanized Astroturf
Gamera
The Gang
Ganglia Dangle
Garmonbozia
Garb Age
Gary's Dim Allegory
Gas Bubble
Gas Comb
Gas Hog
Gas Powered Lips
Gasbag
Gate Crashers
Gato Cabeza
Gawd! I'm A Pancake!
Gawdawful
The Gawkers
Gay Bunting
The Gay Keanus
Gecko Quiver
Gee That's A Large Beetle I
    Wonder If It's Poisonous
Gee That's Swell
The Gee Willikers
Gelatin Explosives
Gelatin Mongoose
General Freak
The Generics

Genghis John
Genital Hospital
Gentleman From Genitalia
Geometric Shapes
Geordi Laforge Can't Get Laid
George Gobel To Block
Geriatric Angst
German Housewives
Geronimo Sours
Get A Terrestrial Life
Get Down On The Ground
Get Lost
Get Out
Get Some Weeding Done
Get That
Get The Phone
Get Well Soon
Getting There From Here
Getting To "Yes"
Getting Up
Ghastly
Ghostly
Ghoti
Giddy
The Giddy Schoolgirls
Giddyup Little Doggie
Gimmick
Ginger And The Snaps
Gingivitis
Gingko Tree
Gingrich
Gipper Hills
The Girl
Girl Scout Heron
Girlie Fries
The Girlie Girls
Girly Maria
Give Me The Knife, Fuckhead
The Gizzards
Glad Cartilage
Glad Hammer
Glad Rags
Glad Tidings
Glaring Omission
Glaring Omissions
Glass
Glass Cameroon
Glass Dick
Glass Of Drano
Glinky Tweebs
Glittering Generalities
Glittery Sticker Fun
Global Thermonuclear War
Glort
Glory Be
Glow-In-The-Dark Stars
Glowing Hot Dog Salmons
Glowing Underwear
Glue Beam
The Glue Factory Rejects
Gnat King Coal
Go Back To Bed
Go Home
Go Play With It Outside
Go Straight To Your Room
Go To College
The Go To The Bathrooms
Goat Model
Gobble
God Baby
God Dammit
God Dog
God Drops You Into The Pit Of Eternal Meat Products
God's Brother
God's Queen
God's Wallet
Godspeed

Going Out Of Business
Going To Japan
The Goings-On
Golf Detective
Gold Baby
The Golden Dedicated Line
The Golden Fleece
The Golden Hind
The Golden Mean
The Golden Rule
Golden Slumbers
Goldfish Peer Pressure
Gomez Sighting
The Goners
Gonna Eat That?
Gonorrhea Pizzeria
Goo Dumbo
Good Band Name
Good Darts
Good Heavens
Good Lord
Good Lord, Choke!
Good News And Bad News
Good Penmanship
The Good Samaritans
Good Word
Goodness Gracious
Goofus And Gallant
Goofy Girl Pizzeria
The Goofy Goo Dumb MC
Goofy's Overalls
The Goons
Gopher's Bow Tie
Gosh
Gospel Bill And The Happiness Drops
The Gothic Toilets
Gotterdammerung
The Gourd Otters
The Government Jobs

Governor Fuzz
Governor Pete
Governor Putz
Gradu
Graily Drind
The Grammies
Gramps
Grand Absolution
Grand Blank
Grand Fusion League
Grand Junction
Grand Mother Fucker
Grand Opening
Grand Theft Auto
Grandpa Jumped Out The Bathroom Window
The Granulations
Granulator
The Grapes Of Moth
Grasshopper Funk
Grav Lax Factor
Gravitational Axes
Gravity Wave
The Great American Novel
The Great Cardiff Giants
Greatest Hits
The Greatly Diminished
The Greatly Preferred
Greed Is Good
Greek To Me
Green Toupee
Greenvelvet
Greeting Card Ninjas
Greetings
Greetings, Earthlings
Gregorian Pants
Grendel
The Grilled Cheeze Fiasco
Grilled Sheep
Grim Imp

Grimace
The Grip
Grist For The Mill
Grisly Bears
Grocery
Groggy
Groovy Wow Songs for Teens
The Gross
Gross Misconduct
Groundhog Skull
Gruesome Boob
The Gruesome Truth
Grunge Harpists
Grunion Minions
Guards! Seize Him!
Guess Your Weight
The Guise
Gulf War Syndrome
Gums And Noses
Gun Patrol
Gunbutt
Gunshy Gumshoe
The Gunslingers
Guttersnipes And Cornerboys
Gutter Loaf
Guyana Koolaid
Guys Who Put Together Vocal Strings And Specific Frequencies For Random Melodies

H

Ha Ha Ha
The Habits
Hacksaw Morons
Haggis Town
Hair Direktor
The Hair And Skin Trading Co.
Hair And Steel
The Hair Of Sam Donaldson
Half A Quorum
Half Duplex
Half Full/Half Empty
Half Off
The Halftones
Halfway To Salem
Hall Of Justice
Ham And Mayonnaise
Ham Salad
Hamburger Blond
Hamburger Butt
Hammered Agog
Hamster Snatchers
Hand Ballet
Hand Wash
Hands Down
Handy 3.5" Disc Cases
Handy Clone
Hanky Panky
The Hanna Barbarians
The Hanseatic League
The Happiest Millionaires
Happiness Is...
Happy And The Horncloggers
Happy And Unhappy Balls
Happy Bag
Happy Birthday

44 / ANDY STURDEVANT

Happy Shiny Naked People
Happy Trunk People
Happyface
Hard Act To Follow
Hard Drive
Hard Into The Wall
Hardware
Hark!
The Harmless Trippers
Harmonic Convergence
Harmonica Armada
Harpoon
Harry And The Hijackers
Harsh Whispers
The Has-Beens
Hat Trick Care Bears
The Haunted
The Have Nots
Have You Any Cheese?
Hawthorne Effect
Hazelnut Twins
He Ain't Dead, He's Just Asleep
He Said She Said
He's Dead Jim
Head Cheese
Head Cheese Whiz
Head Crisp
Head Demagnetizer
Head For The Hills
Head Kelly
Head Like A Pole
Head Rush
Headache
Headache Powders
Headless Torso
Headlice
Headset
Hear No Evil
Hearing Voices
Heat Index
Heavy Balls And The Flip-Offs
Heather Sucks
Heckfire
Hedge Slammer
Hee Haw Hobbit
Hefty Tusker
Heidi Ho
Heinous Aim
Heinous Anus
Heisenberg's Uncertain Tea
The Hellion Killers
The Helicopter Barfs
Hell Destined
Helicopter Meat
Helium-Neon
Hello Larry
Hello, Who Are You And The Globes
Help Wanted
Hemorrhaging
Hepatitis B
Her Breasts Leapt Like Lizards
Here Are The Facts You Requested
Here Goes Nothing
Here's How To Order
Here's Your Stupid Ring Back
Heredity
Heresy
Heresy Fish
Hernia In The Seventh
Hero Worship
Herringade
Heterophobia
Hewlett And The Packards
Hexagon Vex

Hey, Man! What's Up, Dude?
Hey Mister
Hey That's My Bike!
Hey You
Hi Melanie
Hi!
Hiatus
Hickey Party
Hiding Places
High Concept
Highly Avoided
Highway
The Hillbillies
Hippo Cellar
Hiring Freeze
Hiss And Static
The Hissy Fitters
Hissyfit
The Histrionic Toilet Band
Hit The Dirt
Hither And Yon
Hitler Unplugged
Hitting The Head
Hive Queen
Hobblernodge
Hog Wild
Hold For Redefinition
Hold It Right There Mister
Hold The Mayo
Holding Pattern
Holed Up In Montana
Holier Than Mao
Holistic Medicine
Holly Gotta Sucker
Hollywood Chainsaw
Hollywood Enzymes
Holy Bowlers
Holy Cow
Holy Goats
Holy Mackerel
Holy Moly
The Holy Roman Empire
Holy Terror
Holy Wafer Extraction
Homeophobic Remedy
Homework Hotline
Homonymph
Honey Coma
The Honeycomb Centres
Honk If You're Horny
Honky Toast
Honky Tonk Metal Quintet
The Honorable Mention
Hoodlum
Hooker Boy
Hooligan, Ltd.
The Hooligans
Hootie And The Gaspipe
Hoover Hate McCarthy
Hop To It
Hoping For The Best
Horns Of The Crescent Moon
Horse Latitudes
Horse Pills
Horse Vessel
Horse-Drawn Miscarriage
Hostile Varnish
Hot And Bothered
Hot Damn
Hot Plate
Hot Refrigerator
Hot Rod And The Skid Marks
Hot Soup
Hot T'mator Gravy
Hot Tamale
Hot Tip
House Arrest

House Band
House Dressing
House Of Fringe
House Of Wax
Houses In Motion
How About That
How Do You Do
How Grand
How I Loved That Accord And Its Happy Face Pillow
How Much You Bench?
How Nice
How Quaint
Howie Mandel Live!
Hows About That
H.T.M.L.
Huddle Up
Huge Beef Plant
Hugh Watership Downs
Hullaballoo
Hum Drum
Human Karaoke Machine
The Human Race
Human Resources Officer Disco
The Humanoids
The Humble Boaters
The Humpers
Hungrier Than Wilson
The Hungry Alligator Way
The Hunk Of Junk
The Hunnies
The Hunt For Fred October
Hunters And Gatherers
Hurl Jam
Hurling Dairy Products
Hurricane Megan
Huxter
Huzzah
Hydrogen Dumb
Hyena Hijinks

Hygiene First
Hyphen
Hypoxy Pull

I

I Am Stuck In A Band
I Believe In Uncle
I Can't Believe I Ate The Whole Thing!
I Can't Believe It's A Rock Band
I Can't Believe It's Not Better
I Did Not Beat The Rooster
I Don't Feel Fresh
I Don't Know Officer, She Just Died
I Eat The Nacho
I Feed My Anteater On Greenberry Leaves
I Had Wild Jack For A Lover
I Have To Go Out For Something Healthy
I Need Some Healin'
I Paperclipped A Skunk
I See A Great Need
I Shot Hootie
I Was A Teenage Socialist
I Wrote The Bible
I, Mormon
I'd Rather Be In The Cat House Than The Dog House

PARATROOPERS FOR JESUS / 47

I'd Rather Die
I'll Be Damned
I'll Have Another
I'm Not Drunk
I'm With Stupid
I've Got A Bunny
I've Got A Peanut
I've Got A Wedgie
I've Got Cheeks
Ice Cream Headache
Ice Cream Man
Ice Water
Ichabod Wellington and the Jesters Of Destiny
The Ideals
Idée Fixe
Idiotic Jihad
Idle Minds
If I Only Had A Lug Nut
If It Smells Good Eat It
If Pigs Could Talk Would You Still Eat Them
Ill-Fittin' Shoes
The Illegitimatones
The Illuminati
Illusory Illusions
The Immediate Vicinity
Immense Wrapper Torture
Immortal
The Immortal Mortals
Impeach Nixon
Impending Doom
Impersonating Ketchup
The Implants
Important Announcement
The Imprecations
Infantilization
Inflatable Gene Pool
In All Creation
The In Crowd
In Love With Your Mother
In Pursuit
In Spain
In The Bag
In Thine Image
In Transit
In Your Eyes, Officer
The Incidentals
The Incisors
Incoming
Indefinite Discrepancy
Independent Cocoa
Independent Release
The Indignities
The Indiscretions
Individually Wrapped
Induce Vomiting
Induced Vomiting
Industrial Strength
The Industry
Inertial Brunch Factor
Infamouse
The Inferiors
Infield Fly Rule
Infinite Cheese Pizza
The Infinite Pooper
The Infinitoids
Inflammation Age
The Influence
Influence Peddlers
Information Please
Ingrown
Injured Popes
Inkpay Oydflay
Insect Learning
The Insectivores
Insectoid
Insert Slowly
Instant Clout
Instant Coffee

Instruments Of
    Confectionery Discipline
Insufficient Funds
The Insurrectionists
Intake Manifold
Intellectual Masturbation
Intellectual Property
Intensive Care
Inter Alia
Intercap
The Intergalactic Carnival
    Of Sheep
Interlibrary Loan Request
Interlocking Muffin
    Technology
Internal Onions
Internal Revenue Service
International Style
Interrupted Journeys
Intervention Time
The Intimations
Into The Earth
Into The Future
Into The Soup
Intruder Alert
Inversion
Inverting Dreamcake
    Danger
Irene And Her Nuclear
    Pocketbook
The Ironclads
Iroquois Stealth Pilots
Irrational Bankers
Irrational Spike
Irreconcilable Similarities
Irregular Plurals
The Irregulars
The Irresponsible
    Innovators
Irritating Crossfire Weasel

Irritating Noise
Is That Spot's Head?
Isomorph
It All Ends In Tears
It Takes All Kinds
It Would Suck To Be
    A Snake
Its Majesty
It's A Bug And It Hates You
It's Not My Job, Go Ask Jim
It's OK To Slap A Man
It's Payback Time, Santa
It's That Simple
It's Okay, I'm The Pope!
Ixnay

J

Jack Dracula
Jaded Phil
Jailbait Wedding
Jaked Crackers
Jam Yam
The Jamocha Shakes
The Janitor's Problem Now
Janked
The Janky Boys
Jaramillo System
Jasmine Stinks
Jason and the Arguments
The Jazz Baker
Je Suis Une Parapluie
Jed And Jethro
The Jeeps
Jefferson Porn Star Plane

Jello Mold
Jericho Turnpike
Jericho Wall
Jerkwad
Jerry Mander And The Voting Rights Act
Jesse Tree
Jesus Lollipop
Jesus On The Dashboard
The Jesus Presley Experience
Jet Lag
Jewel's Bicycle Seat
Jeweled Carriageway
Jezebel Slick And The Hickeys
J.F.K.F.C.
Jiggety Jank
Jiggle The Clown
Jim Van Morrissey
Jimmy Biscuit And The 10,000 Whining Methodists
The Jinkies
Jinx
Jive Filter
Jive Turkey
Joannie Loves Chachi
Jodhpurs R Us
Joe Puke And The Chunky Bits
Johann Whirlybird
The John Bobbitt Unit
John Denver's Co-Pilot
Johnny Action Finger
Johnny Angel
Johnny Jism
Johnny Vegas
Johnny's Rampin' Ravy Funky Fax
Joker Belly
The Joltin' Jokes
Josetta Floppetta
Juan And The Twos
Judas Hat
Juddhoney
Judo Hairdresser
Juggling Cats
The Juice
Juiceboxology
Juicy Scoop
Julybug
Jumbolove
Jump With Joey
Jumpin' Frogs
Jumpin' Jesus
Jumping Dogs
Jumping Jehoshaphats
Jumpship
Jungle Jerk
Jungle Slut
Junior JFKs
Junior's Problem
Jurassic Storage Co.
The Jury
Just Desserts
Just On Principle
Justice For Ron
Just To Be Cute
Juxtaposer

K

K.A.P.P.
KY Marmalade
Kafka, Franz And Ollie
Kandarin Ebb
Kanji
Kansas U.K.
Kapeesh
Karen's Nicest Dress
Karl Marx Vs. God
Karma Sucre
The Karmatics
Kathie Lee And The Sweat Shops
The Katos
Kay Ann Pepper
Keebler Knob
Keep Going
Keep In Touch
Keep It Down
Keith-Slash-Derek
Kellypan
The Ketchup In Left Field
Key Grip
Kick Me
Kick Me In The Jimmy
Kickin' Ass And The Name Takers
Kicking Buckets
Kid Of Casualty
Kids Of Soup
The Kids Who Never Learned To Color Inside The Lines
Kill Me
Kill Ted Knight
Kill Ya Dead
Killabees
Killer Centerfolds
Killer Kiwis
Killing Me Softly With His Schlong
Kiloton Yield
Kimberly Connection
Kin Shi
The Kind Men Like
The Kind Of People Who Would Drink An Entire Bottle Of Shampoo For $50
Kindercramp
Kinetic Sock Dispenser
King Brown
King Brown Nose
King Wack
Kingdom Of Kush
Kinky Hose
Kiosk
Kiss And Kill
The Kiss Of Death
Kiss The Pyrotechnician
Kiss The Sun
Kisses And Fists
Kissing The Pink
Knab
Knee Deep
Kneecap
Knit That Rip
The Knobby Plunkers
Knowledge Adventure
Kobrinitis
Kooky Munkey
Kow Kountry
Kringle Killers
Krystal Synn
Krystian
Kunk
Kurt Cobain's Dead

Kudzu Acres
Kushy
Kwisatz Haderach

L

The Lab Animals
Labor Day
Laboratory Animals
Lack Of Vision
Lackwit
Lacto-Shack
Lactose Intolerant
Ladder Posse
Ladies Don't Drum
Lady Chatterley's Hamster
Lady Die
Lady Finger Sandwiches
Lady Stick
Ladybug Picnic
Lame Duck Resident
The Lamingtons
Land Of A Thousand Flushes
The Landed Gentry
Landscraper
Lanham Act
Lap Dancer
Lard Filter
Lard-Drivers
The Large And Potentially Dangerous Polygonal Mirror Wheel
Lars Pynwyrm And The Parasites
Las Vegas Lounge Act
Laser Oats
Laserfiend
Lasorda
The Last Drops
Last Great Hamburger
Last Little Chuckle
Last Sonic Dimension
The Last Thing You Wanted to Hear
The Last Word
Latent Buzzard
Lather, Rinse, Repeat
Latitude Bucket Hobbyhorse
Laugh Track
Laughing Gas
Laughingstock
Lawn Dart Accident
Lawn Furniture
The Laws Of Interia
The Laymen
Lead Breakfast
League Leaders
Leaky Bananas
The Leaky Mules
Leather Boxer Shorts
The Leathery Jowls
Le Country
The Left Hand Of God

Legal Aid Society
The Legal And Intellectual Food Chain
The Legendarys
The Lexus Thieves
Leisure Time
The Lemming-Watchers
The Lemon Limes
Lemon Twelve
Leopardskin
Less Than $20
Lesser Known
Let Ringo Sing
Let Us Sand Tomatoes
Let's All Be Flemish
Let's End The War Between The Sexes
Lethal Injection
The Levitating Janitors
Libyan Dills
Lick-A-Wish
Licking Kleenex
Lie Detector
Life And How To Live It
Life As A Fish
Life Incarnate
Life Without Television
The Light Fantastic
Light Year
The Lighthouse Keepers
Lightly Browned
Like A Fish
Like A Rock Band
Like It Or Not
Lima Beans
Limited Time
Limited Time Only
Line Break
Lingering Attitude
Linguistic Confusion
Link Me
The Lip Slobs
Lip Surgeon
Lipstick Sauce
Lipsyncing Fools
Liquid Ice
Liquid Latex
Liquid Reflex
Liquid Street
Liquid Tractor House
Liquorice
Listen Up
The Literate Gibbons
Little Bird
Little Boy Blues Band
Little Freddie
Little Goat
Little Member
Little Sister
The Little Staticky Particles
Little Tickle
Little Timmy
Live On Stage
Live Studio Audience
Living In Squalor
Living Spaghetti
Llama Nuts
Lo-Fi Tempura
Location
Lock And Load
Lockbox
Locker Partner
Locker Room
Loco Cocoa
Logo Rhythm
Lola
London Contemporary Bongo Orchestra
The Lonely Hunters
The Lonely Invaders

Long Distance Dedication
Long Division
Long Drive
Long Hair And Clanging
Longneck
Look At The Artistry Of These Carvings
Look But Don't Touch
Look Closely
The Look At Me Show
Look It Up
Look Out Below
Looking Through Glass
Loophole
Loose Fillings
Loose Pantleg
Loose Threads
Looseleaf Bible
Lord Hepatitis And The Sorry Appetites
Lorena Barbie
Los Angeles Raiders
Los Guys
Los Netanyahus
Losers' Club
Lost Grace
The Lost Profit
The Lost Prophet
Lost Puppy
Lost Sock Found Sock
Lotsa Summery Kisses For Kids Who Live In A Treacle Toffee World
Loud And Obnoxious
Loud Mouse
Louder Than Frogs
Loudmouth
Love A Cricket
Love God Or He'll Kill You
Love Potion No. 9 From Outer Space
Love Smother
Low High
Low Opinion
Lowered Curve
The Loyal Yokemen
Lucid Day
Lucifer Follies
Lucy In Shackles
Lucky Accident
Lucky Stomach
Luftwafer
Lumpy And The Slaw Kings
Lunar Probe
Lunchslut
Lunchline Conspiracy
The Lurk
The Lust Penguins
Lycanthrope
The Lymph Nodes

M

Ma Joad And The Load Blowers
The Machines
Mackerel Thing
Macrowave
Mad At My Shirt

Mad Dash And
   The Hyphenations
Madam, I'm Adam
Made To Order
Magenta Placenta
Magic Kingdom
Magic Number
Magnetic Vacuum
The Magnets
Magnificent Desolation
The Magnificent Font
   Protectors
The Magnificent Letter
The Magnificent Obsessions
Mailing List
Mailman Bites Dog!
Main Course
Majorly Nasty
Make Lisa Rich
Make Way For Willie!
Makes Its Own Gravy
Makin' Bacon
Making Biscuits
Making Haste
Making Noise
Making Real
Malcolm Y
Malcom's Ex
Male Chauvinist Piglets
Malicious Intent
Malignant And The Tumors
Mall Chix
Mallory's Sweater
Malnutritious Food Products
Malt Wink
The Man Downstairs
Man Of The Year
Man With Bra
Manchu Finery
Mandelbrot Sect

The Mandibles
Mangled Meticulous Militant
Mango Munchafella
Manhandle
Manicotti Blizzard
Manifold
Manila Marmadukes
Manson-Nixon Line
Many Moons
The Many Voices Of Hat
Marble Guardians
Marco And The Beast
Marginal Prophets
Maria Girl
Marilyn Manilow
Mario Puzo's Colostomy
   Bag
Mark Twin
Market Pants
The Marks Of Insolence
Maroon Socks
Martha's Boneyard
Martin's Tie
The Martinets
Martinlutherkinks
Mary Jane And The Bongs
Mary Marrow
Mary Unfaithful
Masochistic Aspercreme
Masquerade
Massive Crash And The
   Hispanic Panic Featuring
   DJ Chupacabra
Matching Principle
Math's Hard
The Mausers
Mauve And Life Itself
The Max
Maximum Pudding
May Cause Cancer

May I Help You
May-December Funeral
Maze Of Doom
MC Please And Thank You
Me And My Fun-Lovin' Pinto
Me Lucky Charms
Me Quite Dumb
Me Three
Me Too
Me, Myself, And Eye
Mealworm
The Means
Meany Heads
Meat Beatles
Meat By-Product
Meat Hat
Meat Is Yummy
Meatpipe
Meatplow
Median Strippers
The Mechanicals
Media Professional
Medium Dice
Medium Rare
Meerkats
Meet The Band
Mega Smegma
Megadesk
Melatonin
Melissa's House Of Crabs
The Melodramatics
Meltdown
Melodious Thunk
The Membranes
The Men
Men Against Retirement
Men And Women
The Men Who Knew Too Much
Men's Fragrance
Menial Task

Menstrual Yogurt
Mercurial
Mesopotamian Hippopotamus
Messiah's Handle
Metal Roses
Methane Tower
Method Amphetamine
Methodists To The Madness
Metric Day
The Metric Program
Michael And The Molesters
Mickey Mantle's Liver
Microbaby
Microluminesecent
Microwave Reincarnation
The Middle Of Nowhere
Midwife Crisis
MiG Sphincter
Mighty Moose
Mile-High Super Sloth
Milk Gel
Milksop Aesop
Millenium Sparrow
Mimekill
Mimeograph
Mind Prophet
Mine Shaft Gap
Mini-Large
Miniskirt Fetish
Miniature Golf
Minimum Wage
Minister
Mint Spy
Mirror Image
Misery Device
Misfits Of Science
Misguided Attempts
Misnomer
Miss Hitler
Miss Misanthrope

The Missing Sink
Mission Control
Mission To Mars
Mistaken Identity
The Mister Men
Misthaufen
Mixed Bag
Mixed Drinks
The Mixed Metaphors
Mixed Signals
Mmmmm, Soup!
Mob Psychology
Mock Frog
Moderation
Modern Civilization
Modern World
Modulation
Moe-Moe
Moist Fist
Moist Tips
Moldy Steak
Moldy Toe
Molly Pill
Mom Bomb
Mom on Bass
Mom On The Crapper
Mom! You're Turning Punk?
Mommy Don't Let Your Kids Join The Sanhedrin
The Monads
Mondale's Revenge
Money-Back Guarantee
Mongolian Goat Beard
Monkey Do
Monkey Don't
Monkey Dump
Monkey Fucks Football
Monkey Girl
Monkey Has One Eyebrow
Monkey's Uncle
Monkeybird
Monkeys In The Zoo
The Monroe Doctrine
Monster Trucks
The Monsters
Moo Car
Moo Juice
Moo Money
Mood Music
Moodswings
Moonshine Willy
Moosetooth
Moral Standards
The Moravian Tube Throwers
The Morbid Tavern Apple Choir
Morbidous Pathology
Morde du Temps
More Crap
More Or Less Remarkable
More Than Muffins
More Spock Music
Moribund Bellfrey
The Morlock From Porlock
Mormons From Other Planets
The Morning After
Morning In Morocco
Moron Envy
Moron Victim
Mortuary Wreath
Mosetti Katunga
Moshing Millipedes
The Most Beautiful Cephalopod
Moth Loader
Mother And The Tuckers
Mother Bucks
Mother Haters

Mother Knows Best
Mother Load
Mother Outlaw
Mother's Cajolery
Mound
The Mouth Of Zeus
Mouthful Of Ashes
Move Over Bacon
Move Over Boomer
Mr. Holland's Anus
Mr. Juice
Mr. Machine
Mr. Nelson
Mr. Pissed-Off-His-Nut
Mr. Precedent
Mr. Ridiculous
Mr. Shit
Mr. Tangent
Mr. Wet Noodle Got A Woody
Muck And Mire
Muffin Man
Muffin Messiah
Mugwump
The Mugwumps
Multiple Stab Wounds
Mumbo Jumbo
The Muncie Indianans
Muscat And Oman
Mussolini's Picnic
Mustard Gas
The Musts
Mutant Glaze
The Mutated Daisies I Once Found In My Garden
The Muttonchops
Mutual Funds
My Atomic Bomb
My Big Spoon
My Charming Assistant

My Dad Lost Twenty Pounds
My Ex-Boyfriend's Accountant
My Father's A God
My Friend Bubba
My Gravity Well Has Run Dry
My Life In Cartoons
My Mother, The Deuce
My Oh My
My Other Band Is A Three-Piece Combo
My Pet Cow
My Principal Makes Peanuts
My Retching Sociopath
My Second-Favorite Martian
My So-Called Death
My So-Called Wife
My Town Selectman
My Wheels Are Falling Off
Myasthma
The Myrrh
The Myst Junkies
Mysteries Of The Unknown
Mystery Achievement
Mystery Collection
Mystery Movie
Mystic Swiss Knives

N

Nailed To The Floor
Naked Barbie
Naked David Hasselhoff
The Naked Guys
Naked Nun
Naked Potato
The Naked Skinnies
Namby-Pamby
Name Taken
Name That Smell
Nameless Terror
Nancy's Back
Narcoleptic Waffle Dodgers
Narrow Margin
Nasal Blockage
Nash Rambler And The Spare Parts
Nat King Colon
Nation Of Actuaries
Nation Of Isn't
National Pornographic
The National Splits
National Time Signal
Natural Gas Nipple
Nature's Sunken Wreck
Naughty Money Girls
Naughty Toddler
Naval Fungus
The Nazi Beatles
Nazi Christmas
The Necessaries
Necropsy
Ned Rennet, Secret Spy
Need Another Name
Needle In The Red
Needle Nose
Needle To The Red
Needlenose
Needless Wheedling
The Negaters
Negative Charge
Negative X
Negativity
Nematode Twist
Nemesis
The Neo-Luddites
Neo-Velvets
Neon Eaters
Neptune
Netherken
Netminder
Network Failure
Never Wrong
New! Improved!
New Age Facilitator Man
New Balance
New Boots
New Car Smell
New Fall Season
The New Gothics
New Media Assault
The New Revisionists
The New Switcheroo
New Tricks
The New Victims
The New You
News Media Types
Newt!
Next Exit
Next To Earl
Niblets
Nice Crater, Einstein
The Nice Girl Position
Nice Legs
Nice Try
Night Fighters

Night Shift
Nightshade
Nine Inch Hangnails
Nine Karma Nine
Nipples Of Venus
Nirvanarama
Nirvanica
The Nit-Pickers
Nitrogen
No Big Loss
No Comment
No Contest
No Dessert
No Dumping
No Fun For Kids
No Harm Done
No Lead Is Safe
No Longer With Us
No Money Down
The No Names
No One In Particular
No Pain, No Gain
No Sex Before Lunch
No Survivors
No Transfer
No Way Jose
The No-Tones
Noband
Nobody's Friend
Nocturnal Urinals
Noize II Men
Nominal Plant
Non-Mongol Horde
Non-Deliverables
Non-Famous Sons Of Martin Sheen
Nonconformist Uniform
The Noncommittal Grunts
None Of The Above
None Too Soon

Nonfamily
Nonresponse
Norm!
The Normally Urbanes
Northern Spies
Northern Belle
Nose Dive
Nose Miners
Not Animal Tested
Not As Good As Ezra
Not At All
Not For Profit
Not Here Yet
Not In Service
Not My Spoon
Not The Man You Married
Not Tonight
Not Unlike Lazarus
Not Very Not
Not Yet Ripened Ones
Note Paper Jezaz
Nothing
Nothing New
Notline
Notoriously Sullen
Novelist
Now Look Here
Now That's An Autopsy!
Now What
Nowhere Eleven
Noxious Humours
Noxious Turd
Nuance Shock
Nuclear Dog Food
Nuclear Easter Egg
Nuclear Emissions
Nuclear Family Accident
Nuclear Minds
Nuclear Puppet
Nuclear Tide

Nude Fruit
Null Hypothesis
Number-One Jaywalker Death City
Number Please
Nuremberg Milkshake
Nutritious Minds
Nuts Can Surf
Nylon Accident

O

O'Constitution
The O.K. Bombers
O.B.G.Y.N.
O.J. Did It
Oasis 2
The Oath
Objects In Mirror
Objective Blowjob
Oblong Patent
Obscene Spandex
Obstructed Airway
Obstructed Sink
Obvious Intentions
Obviously Sucks
Ocarina Jamboree
Occam's Barber
Occasionally Tough People
Odd Bodkin And The Thousand Gadzooks
Odd Lot

The Odds Are Against Us
Oddsmakers
Oedipus and the Mama's Boys
Oedipussy
Of A Pin
Of Dreams
Off Like A Prom Dress
Off Limits
The Offending Foot
Offensive Sugary Globules
Official Document
Officer Jeffrey T. Gillespie, 26
Oh Boy
Oh Come Now
Oh For Pete's Sake
Oh Great
Oh Hell
Oh The Humanity
Oh You're Home
Oh!
Oklahoma Glaucoma
Okra Club
Old Gord And The Purple Clouds
Old Paint
The Old Switcheroos
Oligopoly
Olly Olly Oxen Free
Omaha Beach
Omega Plum
The Omen Drones
On All Fronts
On Location
On The Brink
On The Fritz
On The Money
On The Piss
On The Rocks

PARATROOPERS FOR JESUS / 61

One Big Stack
One Body Too Many
One Inch Speakers
One Night Only
One Or The Other
One Too Many
One Word Alternative Band Name
One-Eyed Stiffy
One-Eyed Willy And The Water Weasels
One-Man Industry
One-Week Paid Sodomy Vacation
Only Words
Oprah's Book Club
Ophrastitution
Oo-Wee
Ooh. Ouch!
The Oolites
Oolong Tea Boy
Oops
Ooze Juice
Open Bar
Open Daily For Breakfast
Open Other End
Open-Door Policy
The Opening Act
Operators Are Standing By
Opportunity Wasted
Optional Music
Orange Crush
Orange Roughy
Orange Sauce
Orator Jim
Orchestra
Order By Phone
Order Now
The Organ Donor Grinders
Orbiting Stars
Oregon Book Of The Dead
Oreo Speedwagon
Orgy Of Silence
Orifice Swapmeet
The Original Celebrated Curiously Hardcore Band
The Original Darrens
The Original Piece Of Shit Band
Oscar's Trash Can
Oscillation On The Scope
The Other Hand
The Other Rolling Stones
Ottoman Empire
Ouagadougou
Ouch
Ouchy Mama
Our Instruments Are Useless
Our Lady Of Perpetual Hangtime
Our Mother's Pride
Our Neighbors To The North
Our Porcine Friends
Out Of Control
Outburst
The Outcome
Outhouse Critic
Outrage
Ovarian Trolley
Ovarydose
Oven Bake
Over And Over
Overall Effect
Overuse Of Energy
The Overdone
Overload
Oxen House
Oxy Overdose
Oxyacetylene

P

The Pace
Pachinko Pacino
Pacific Rimjobs
Package Deal
Packard Jell
Packing Tacos
Page-Down
Pain Go Bye-Bye
Pain Go Bye-Bye Juice
Pain Threshold
Painful Urination
Paint A Saint
Paisley Brain Cells
Pajama Jo
Palatino 12
Palm Pilot
Pampaluga
The Pampered Dandies
The Pamphlets
Pan Fight Nightly
Pan-Blackened Dog Nose
Panasonic Youth
Pancake Planet
Pancreas Trap
Panda Summons
Pandanistas
Pangaean Senate
Panoply
Paper Clip Massacre
Paper Or Plastic?
Parabola
Parade Of Pearls
Paraesthesiae
The Parameters
Paramour Pink
Paratroopers For Jesus
The Parsons
Parting Gifts
Partly Cloudy
Partridges In The Pear Tree
Party Hats And Tater Tots
Parvovirus
Pasadena Roof-Top
Pascal's Quadrangle
Pascal's Triangle
Pascal's Wager
Pastoral Abyss
Pastrami And The Salad
Pasty White Thighs
Pathogen
Pathos Of Least Resistance
Patliners
Patootie
Patronizing News Professional
Pattern Finder
Paul McCartney Will E-mail Us
Paul Will Eat Himself
Paul's Interview
Pavlov's Master
Pay At The Door
Pay Dirt
Pay-Per-View
Peace Riot
Peachy Preachers
Peanut Butter Cup
Peasants With Pitchforks

Pearl Drops
The Pedantic Philosophers
	Of Lent
Pedestrian Hominy
Pegasaurus
The Pee Pee Whackers
Pee Shy
Pee-Bop
The Peekers
Peel The Chicken
Peer Pressure
Pelican
Pegleg Sexy
The Penetrating Analyses
Penile Exudate
Pentagram Attempt
Penthouse Bunnies
People Of Earth
People Persons
The People Who Brought
	You Last Week's #1 Single
The People Who Live In
	The Trees
Peppered
Per Ivars
Per Se Violation
Perceptual Object-Mediator
Perfect Oval
Perforated Head
Perkler Manson
Perky Rhombus
	And The Point
Permanently Pressed
Permian Swamp
Permission Denied
Perms For Pensioners
Peroxide
Perplexed
Persian Dupe
Personal Hygiene

Personality Transplant
Pest Control
Pestilence Of The Damned
Pestillent Fax
The Pests
Peter Lies Here
Peter Panphage
Peter, Petere, And Petar
Peter Pornomaker
Petits Fours
Petrol Blivet
Petroleum Juggernauts
pH Balanced For Women
Phalanx
Phantom Limb
The Phenomenon
The Philbins
The Philistines
Phillips
Phlegmatic Response
The Phone
Phone Bill From Hell
The Phonies
Phorm
Phosphorus Bomb
Photo Auction
Physical Tim
Picard's Earl Grey Enema
Pick It Up
Picklelicious
Pickled Sinners
Pickled Torso
Pier 666
Pierced Goatee
Pig Dipper
Pig's Arse
Pigs In A Poke
Pigs In Blankets
Pigs in Heaven
Pillars Of Leaden Agony

Pillar Assault
Pillow-Stealing Ninjas
Pilot Light
The Piltdown Men
Pimps Of Venus
Pinched Nerve
Ping Machine
Pinhead Circus
Pink Eye
Pink Giant Ninnies
Pink Ink
Pink Jesus
Pink Taco Disease
Pink Tammy
The Pirated Dreidels
Piso Mojado
The Piss Ants
Piss Drunk
Piss Fit
The Pissflaps
Pistachio Fluff
Pistol Whip
Pizza Slut
The Pizzeria Tarts
Placental Goulash
Plague Of Salesmen
Plaid Sabbath
Plaid Sector
Planet Of Pants
Planet Red
Planned Patenthood
Plastic Bimbette
Plastic Bust
Plastic Cow Snack
Plastic Cows
Plastic Crap
Plastic Fajita
Plastic Ghost
Plastic Jubilee
Plastic Little

Plastic Pants Au Gratin
Plastic Passion
Plastic Plants
Plastic Santa Claus
Playing Bingo On A Waffle
Playing In Traffic
Playmate of the Year
Please Identify
The Pleasing Shimmers
Pleated Spleen
Plexus
Plink Aplenty
Ploo
Plot Complication
Plus Tax
Plutonium
Po'bucker Dilemma
Poetic License
Poetry Spring Shoot
Point And Click
Pointy Bra Years
Poisoned Oasis
Poision Phlegm
The Poison Toads
Poke
Poker Party
Polar Baby
Policy Makers
Polka Geeks
Pollution
Pomplamousse
Poo Chiclets
Poo Juice
Poo Poo Faces
Poof Like That
Poonanie Cramp-Up
Poop Soup
Poop-Tarts
Poopy Cupcake Wizards
Pop Ate Itself

Pop Quiz
Pop Secretions
Pop Shop
Popcorn Pencils
Popcorn Pimp
Pope Fiction
Pope John Paul Quartet
Popemobile
Popper
Poppin' Fresh
Popsky
Poptart Hippos
The Popular Demands
Porcelain God
Porch Girls
Porcine Candor
Porcupine Racetrack
Porcupine Slit
Pork Products
Pork Sensation
Porky Prig
Port Of Batavia
Portable Dental Floss Crue
Portable Hula Hoop
Portable War Memorial
Posiedon's Pyros
Posh
Possum Pie
Post-Acoustic Syndrome
Post Nasal Drip
Post No Bills
Post Office Massacre
The Postgrads
Postmatrimonial Void
Postmodern Suggestion
The Potato Papists
Potato Power
Potato Punch
Potpourri
Potsie Loves Chachi

Potty Seat
Pound Foolish
Pound Signs Of
  The Apocalypse
Poundcake
Pout
Powder Magazine
Powder Toes
Powdered Water
Power Glove
Power Of Attorney
The Power Of Positive
  Thinking
Power Play
Power Spectrum
Pox On Thee
Prairie Gothic
Praise Cheeses
Preacher Roe
Prealpha
Predilection
Pregnant In A Miniskirt
Prehistoric Peter
  And The Dimetrodons
Premadonna
Premature Circular Boy
Premature Evacuation
The Prescription Drugs
The Present Tense
President Bongo And
  Friends
President Rodman
The Prestons Always Were a
  Bit Twitchy
Presumed Missing
Pretty Accident
Pretty Colors
Pretty Good Chance
Pretty Lady At The Terminal
Prevarication Integration

Prevent The Future
Previous Life
The Price Is Wrong
Prime Directive
Prime Meridian
Primeval Ministers
Primitive Ancestry
The Prince Who Was Formerly An Artist
Princess Banana
Principal Killa
Printed Lining For Privacy
Prisms Dot My Screen
Prison Date
Prisoner's Dilemma
The Pro-Creators
Probiscus
Pro-Breast
Process R2-45
Proctor Logical
Product Placement
Product Recall
Professor Morrison's Lollipop
The Profit Margins
Project Jake
Projectile Discharge
Projector Screen Deficit
Prolonged Silence
The Prom Dates
The Promiscuous Soldiers
Promise Not To Laugh
Promissory Estoppal
The Proofreaders
Prop 13
Proteus
Protozoid
Proxy
Prozac Achievers
The Prozac Experience
Prozac Princess
Psychic Friends Network
Ptomaine Toes
Public Catharsis
Public Cleats
Public Enemy Limited
Public Hair
Public Quandary
Public Safety
Public Speaking Display
Public Spectacle
Puce
Puce Hubert
Puck Stocking
Pudhoney
Puff
Puke Toothpaste
Pull My Finger
Pull My Finger Chili Cookoff
Pumice
Pumpernickel
Pumpkin Goo
Punctuate As Necessary
The Punctuations
The Pundits
Pungent
Punic War
Punish With Love
The Punted Buns
Pup Eraser
Pure
Pure Bliss
Pure Enjoyment
Purely Rotten
Purgatory
Puritan Pukes
Purple Clairvoyance
The Purple Funk
Purple Moon
Purple Whig

Pushbutton Matrix Option
Pustulent Favorite
Putty
Putty Top
Puzzling Evidence
Pyjama Joe
Pyrex Clerk
Pyrrhic Victory

Q

Quack
The Quadrilaterals
Quadrycycle Mobile
Quality Control
Quality You Can Taste
Quartz Spider
Quayle For President
Queen And The Deadbeat Dads
Quench
Quentin Quite
Questionable Practices
Quickly
Quicksand Skinnydipping
Quik And Hide
Quite A Din
The Quivering Fat Band
Quorum
Quote Unquote

R

Rabbit Flats
Radar Range
Radio Fool
Radio Judas
Radio Riot
Radio Shirt
Radioactive Watermelon Eaten With A Spoon
The Radios
Rage Against Mr. Clean
Rage Against The Eugene
The Rain
Rainbow Wig Gifford
Rainchecks
Raisin Days
Rake Freak
Raking It In
The Rakish Boutonnieres
Ramblin' Grammas
The Rampaging Hippies
Rancid Liberals
The Random Band Name Generators
Random Dudes
Random Weirdness
Randomized Lobotomy
The Rankards
Ranklefeather
Rappin' Rats
Rasputin's Beard

Raspwagon
Rasslin' With Yer Dog
Ratings Points
Ratio Killers
Rats Of Unusual Size
Raunch Dressing
The Raving Puss-Heads
The Razor's Edge Plan
The Razorblade Sandwiches
Reach For The Ceiling
The Reactors
Reagan On Rye
The Reagan Years
The Reagents
Real Estate Agency
Real Human Beings
Real Live Dead Bodies
The Real Lovers
Real World
Really Bad Food
Reap
The Reaper's Daughter
Reasonable Pathogen
Rebus
Receding Hairline At 16
Receivership
Recent Farm
Recharge
Reckless Recluse
Reconfigured
Record Industry
Recovery Team
Rectum Tangle
Red Alert
Red Eft
Red Flying Addicts
Red Herring
Red House
Red Manila
Red Meat Bears Fruit
Red Salmon In A White Wine Sauce
Red Shift
Red Star
Red Tsunami
Redback
Redneck International Airport
The Refined Wonderbred
Reflective Viking Fish
Refunds And Exchanges
Reggae Death Squad
Registered Voters
Regression
Rehab
Reindeer Barbecue Days
The Rejects
The Relators
Releasing Methane Fumes
The Reliquaries
The Reluctant Astronauts
Remember The Maine
Renaissance, Man
Rent With Cancer
Renting Out My Skull
Reported Incident
Reprint
Republican Dirty Tricks
Rerelease
The Reservations
Reserve Officers' Training Pants
The Residuals
Residue Existence
Restimulate
The Restless Are Native
Restraining Order
Restricted Area
Resumes Featuring Salary
Retaliation

Retellings Of Cherished
  Classics
Retilt The Head
Retrieve From Bottom
Retro Gnome
Retrograde
Return For Deposit
The Reuben Kinkaid
Revelation In Reason
Reverend Houseplant
Reverend Ron And The
  Revolving Doors
Rhesus Monkey Cups
Rhino Sex
Rhinohumpers
Rhymes With Orange
Rhythmic Overdose
Ribbed For Her Pleasure
Richard's Nixon
The Richards
Ricki BBQ
The Ridiculoids
The Right Connections
The Right To Refuse Service
Right-Wing Lighthouse
  Graffiti
Righteous Nitrous
The Righteous Queries
The Rim
Ripley's Phaser
Ripoff
Rising Influence
Rising Scum
Risky Grownup Movies
Roadkill On The Highway
  To Heaven
Roadkillers
Roadside Abortion
Roaring 20
Roaty Toaty Scrotum

Robber Barons
Robot Friends
Rock 'N' Roll Watermelons
Rock 'N' Roll For Dummies
Rock Bottom
Rock Cornish
Rocket Fool
Rocket Pop
Rockin' Horse
The Rocking Dildos
Rocky Mountain High
Rod And The Furlongs
Rodent System
Roger That
The Roiling Boil
Rolling Donut
Roman Frenz And
  the Countrymen
The Roofies
Room With No View
Root Doctors
Rootettes
Rotary Vent
Rotator
The Rotators
Rote Joy
Rotten Tomato Meets Butt
Rough Towels
The Row
Royal Fun Force
Royal Mango Boys
The Rub
Rub A Baby Buggy Bumper
Rubber Dumplings
The Rubber Matches
Rubber Orange Factory Girls
The Ruckus
Ruckus Amok
Rug Burns
Rug Carpet Torch Muffin

Ruined Forever
The Rum Runners
The Rumbelles
Run Don't Walk
Run For It
Runaway Meatball Wagon
Runes Of Monaco
Runk Pock
Running Mates
The Rustic Moon Bags
Rusty Nail
Rutabaga Bag

S

The Sacramentals
Sacred Anomaly
Sacred Cow
Sacred Meatball Lasagna
The Sad Bastards
Sad Girl
Sad Little Morph
Sad Little Sex Life
Safe And Sound
The Safe And Sound
Sailing With Maari
Saints Preserve Us
Sales Pitch
Salesmen Of A Divine Nature
Sally Jessie Ralph Like Hell
Salvador Daddy
The Same Old Band
Sample Size

San Francisco Treat
San Juan Hal
Sandbox Pimp
Sanity Napkins
Santa Pants
Santa's Pudding Pop
Santa's Pyjamas
Sap Factory
Sap Sucker
The Sarariman Implodes
Sarcophagus
Sassafras
Sassafrassy
Satan Day
Satan Worshippers With Curvy Knives
Satan's Death Boner
Satan's Older Sister
Satanic Teenage Timebombs
Satanic Vibes Of Death
Satanica
The Satin Worshipers
Saturated Fat
Saturday Night Beaver
Saturday's Garbage
Sausage Juice
The Savages
Save The Whales
Sawhores
The Scabrous Leeks
Scallion Boot Camp
Scheduled Maintenance
Schlong
Schtick In The I
Schwa With An Umlaut
Science Experiment
Science Monitor
Scimitar
Sclera

Scooby's Doos
Scorch
Scoreless
Scotch Guard
Scoundrel
Scourge
Scram
Scramble
Scrape Gently
Scrappy Doo
Scratch 'N' Sniff
Scratch-N-Sex
The Screamin' Freemen
The Screaming Abe Vigodas
Screaming Engines In Space
Screaming Licorice Bits
Screaming Veals
The Screaming Yodelers
Screen Credit
Screwtop Messiahs
Scripture Spew
Scrod Tonic
Scrotum Poles
Scrumpy
Scully And Mulder's Favorite Year
Sea Wasp
Seat Thickener
The Second Thing
Sea Of Crises
Search Engine
Season Ticket
Second Warning
Secondary Sexual Developments
Seconds from Destruction
Secret Charm
Secret Drunk
The Secret Identity of Colonel Mustard
The Secret Naughty Pleasures
The Secret Rabbis
Secret Recipe
Secret Touching Game
The Secretions
Section 43 Violation
Section Seven
Security Clearance
Sediment House
Sedimentary Layer
See Spot Run
Seeds And Stems
Seedy Romz
Seeking Preparations
Self Castration
Self-Cleaning Ovens
Self-Propelled Mask
The Self-Righteous Brothers
Senator
Send Help
Senility
Senior Citizen Shot-Put Practice
Senior Discount
Sensitive Orgy
The Sensuous Paperboys
Sentimental Gentlemen
Sequel Police
Sequestered Juror
Serendipity Blow Torch
Serotonin Psychonaut
Serrated Edge
Services Rendered
Serving Suggestion
Seth Nable
Seven 7

Seven Circles
Seven El Elvis
Seven-Letter Word
Seventh Day Adventurists
The Seventh Juggling Seal
The Seventies
Several Beverages
Severed Hand And The Twitches
Severely Enlarged Fish
Sex And The Single Girl
Sex Girl Patrol
Sexist Pigs
Sexquilibrium
Sexual Crisis
Shad Roe And The Gars
Shade Dock
Shagbark
Shaken Not Stirred
Shakes Beer
Shakin' Baby Syndrome
Shallop
Sham Fantasy
Shamash
The Shambles
Shape Of Things To Come
Sharon Stoner
Sharp Dressers
Sharpshooter
Shasty Daisy
Shat
Shazam
She'll Take This Seriously
She's In New York
Sheep In A Drum
Sheesh!
Shi-Tzu Love
Shifting Spanner
Shifty's Rocket
Shiny Yellow Mom

Shit Bong
Shit Smell
Shit-Spangled Banner
The Shitkickers
Shitty Shitty Band Band
Shock Sonata
Shocken
Shoot That Laserbeam
Shoot Them
Shootin' Fish In A Barrel Of Monkeys
Shoots Flaming Balls
Shorn Like Bjorn
Short Fuse
Short Shrift
Short Walk Off A Long Pier
Shortstop Of The Future
Shot At Sunrise
Show Us Your Tits
Shower Very Carefully
Shrug
Shucha Trap
The Shucks
Shut Up Shuttin' Up
The Shy Mercenaries
Sick And Tired
Sick Ed
Sick In Bed
Sick Little Monkey
Sick My Duck
The Sickly Seven
Side Project
Sideband
Sidereal Vectors
Sideways Eight
Sidewinder
Sign Of The Triple-Finned Hammerhead
Signal 20
Silent Groove

The Silent Jazz Ensemble
Silent Letters
Silent Mimes
Silent Stick Phreaks
Silk Sheets
Similar Jones
Simon's Dilemma
Simple Men
Simple Semolina
Simulated Orgasms
Simulcast
Simultaneous Translation
Sinful Child
The Single Greatest Force Of Evil On Earth
The Singularity
Sissy Spaceshot And The Solar Garlics
Sisters Of Morrissey
Sitting Duck
Six Figures
Six More Sins to Go
Six Shooter Gun And A One Shooter Knife
Sizzling Monkeys
Skanky
Skeletor Association Of America
Sketch Comedy
Ski Warthog Dive Bar Bud
Skin Gone Bad
Skin-So-Soft UK
Skinhead Protocol
Skinny Bastard
Skip Collection
Skipping A Beat
Skivvies, Pastrami And Corn
Sklar
The Skraelings
Skullbuggery
The Skullcaps
Skunkweed
Sky-High
Slam-Crash
Slap Back That Fat
Slap In The Face
Slaughterhouse
Sleep Like A Baby
Sleep Station
Sleeper Hit
Sleepflower
Sleeping Bow Tie
Sleeping Dogs Lie
Sleeping With The Enema
Sleepyhead
Slicker Than Slick
Sliding Hiatus Hernia
Slim Porridge And The Dirty Birds
Slim Profile
Slimy Bean Dish
Slimy Goat People From Louisville
Slings And Arrows
Slippery People
The Slipping Mickies
The Slithy Toves
Slob Network
Slobberknockers
Sloch
Sloppy Free
Slosh
Slouch
Slow Trucks
Slumber Party Massacre
Slump
The Slut Brothers
Slut Cola
Smart Antelope
Smart Lenny

Smash And Grab
Smashing Crows
Smashing Guitars
Smegma
Smell Michael
Smell Of Bacon
The Smell Of God
Smelliferous Orbs Of Feminine Pleasure
Smells Like Bakersfield
Smells Like My Dentist's Office
Smiling Toenails
Smite
Smoke Wagon
Smoking For Lyle
Smoking Pac-Men
Smuckey
Smug Musings
Smuggler
Smurfkiller
The Snakefest Of Reasoning
Snakemate
Snap Out
Snappy Mathematics
Sno-Cones From Heaven
Snorting Detergent
Snot-Assed Warthogs
Snotty Allure
Snow Pants
Snowblind
Snowfox Tumblers
Snuff The Ficus
Snugglepusses
So Delightful
So I Says To Him If You Want A Band Name You Better Think Of One Yourself
So Precious
So Sue Me
So To Speak
So You Want To Be A Presbyterian
Soap Dish
Sober Alcoholics
Society For The Protection of Alternative Music
The Sociopaths
Sodium Content
Sofar
Soggy Boxers
Soiled
Soilmaster
Solar Dust
Solar Shuttle
Solid Waste
Solig
Solo Act
Solomon's Porch
Solution Factor 67
Soma Time!
Somber Existence
Sombre Reptiles
Some Killjoy
Some Local Band
Some People's Kids
Some Small Ordinary Things And The Table They Sit On
Sometain Certhing
Something Blatant
Something In A Bucket
Something Is Wrong Here
Something To Do
Something's Got To Give
Sometimes I Squeeze The Cheese, Sometimes The Cheese Squeezes Me
Sometimes This
The Somewhat Perplexed

The Somnambulators
Son Of Ethel
Son Of Son
Sonic Boom
Sonic Explosion
Sooey
Sophisticated Mousehole
Sophomore Jinx
Sordid Retort
Sore Thumb
Sorry
Sorta Like Chicken
Sound Flounder
Sound Prisoners
Sounds Of Beta
The Soup Cookies
The Soup Kitchen
Soupstick
Sour Nation
Sour Shitter
South Of The Border
Soviet Pie
Space Corporation
Space Pets
The Spaces
Spackle
Spacklecore
Spam Cell
The Spam Hurts
Spam Is A Registered Trademark
Spamliners
Spandex Mommy
Spankme Delano Roosevelt
Spanish French And The Viennese Norwegians
Spankings And Salvation
Spare No Quarter
Sparky the Chickendog
Spatial Forces
Spatula Jim And The Flap Jacks
Speakeasy
Speaking Basque
Speaking Of Bisque
Spearhead
Special Guest
Special Lenses
Special School
Spectacular Failure
The Spectators
The Spencers
Spent Casings Of Discarded Friends
Spermicidal Tendencies
Sphinx
The Spice Must Flow
Spidel Ident
Spider Fine
Spider Lake Miracle Shrine
The Spider's Stratagem
The Spielbergs
Spike And The Nines
The Spillover Effect
Spillway
Spinning Squirrels
Spiral Trance
Spiritual Crisis
Spirograph
The Spit Rumba Folk Hour
Splat
The Splendids
The Splendor That Was Athens
Splintered Toes
Splinters
Splitting Headache
S.P.L.O.O.G.E.
Splotch
Spock In Chains

Spock's Blood
Sponge Bath
Sponge Fisherman
Sponge Puppet
Sponge Trap
Spoon Chatter
Spotty Browns And The Elixir
Spread
Spreadem
The Spreading Rumors
The Spree Killers
Spring Sprockets
Spruce Pundit
Spunk Gutter
Spurned Idols
Squab Follies
Square Frogs
Square Peg And The Dog House
Squash Bucket
Squawking Box
Squeak
Squeaking By
Squeaky Freak
The Squeamish Squids
Squeezed
Squeezing Cheese
Squelch
Squid Jiggin' Union Local 304
Squid-Shaped Sid And The Appendages
Squirming Cheesefood
Squirrel Jockeys
Squirt
The Squirtin' Grapefruits
The Squirts
St. Swithen's Day Parade
Stabitty Stabitty Stab Stab
Staccato Surprise
Stack The Deck
Stackpole
Stadium Way
Stag Film
Stage Fright
Stage Left
Stage Two
Stale Beer
Stale Comet
Stalking Bambi
Standard Issue
Stanley Planet And His Throbbing Unit
Star Meets Star
Staring At The Sun
Stark Naked
Stars On Colt .45
State Department
State Pen
Staunch Suppporters
Stay Away
Stay Of Execution
Staying Out Of Trouble
Steak Skirt
Stench Heaven
Step To The Plate
Sterile Ferrets
Stern Dozen
Stew Jubilee
The Stewed Prunes
Sticker Shock
Stickmen
Sticks And Bones
Sticky Zipper
Stiff Muscles
Stillframe
Sting, You Pretentious Bastard
Stinkwatch

Stinky Dave With His Shirt Off
Stinky Fire Engine
Stipend
Stir Crazy
Stolen Arc
Stone Age Bimbo
Stone Conscience
Stone Moses
Stoner Mike Wallace
Stools For Sale
Stop Me Up
Stop That
Stop The Insanity
Stop The Press
Stop! It's Cafeteria Food!
Stork Orchestra
Storyline
The Straight And Narrow
Straining Saliva
Strange Attractor
Strange Jacket
Strange Ways
Strapping Young Men
Street Cred Catastrophe
Street Liquid
Strewn Giant
Strict Liability
Strike
Strike Discord
Strikeout Victims
Strip Battleship
Strip Poker
Stronger Than Dirt
Strum Of Consciousness
Strung Out
Strychnine On The Side
Stuck In Goo
Stuck In The Mud And Making Out
Studded Rubber Nubs
The Student Body
Studio Chiefs
Stuff
Stuffinsuch
Stunned Mouse In A Dixie Cup
Stunt
Stupefaction
Stupid Concrete
Stupid Lifestyle Choices
The Stupidheads
The Style Otters
Style Tax
Subcutaneous Garbanzo
Subdeb
Subject, Verb And Object
Subliminal Maryanne
Submission
Subsequent Norman
Subsonic
Subterranean Currency
Subterranean Vault
Subtle Alert
Suburbia
The Subway Oysters
Sucker Ball
The Suckers
Suckin' on a Tweeter
Sucking Diction
Sucking Hugh Grant
Suction Cup Face
Sugarsmack
Suicidal Grunge Rockers
Sumpin'
Sunglasses For Jimmy
Sunny Tunic
Sunshine Alice
Super Smashing Lovely
Superb Doom

Superdrug
Superman In A Box
Supersmack
Supreme Executive
Supreme Soviet
Surely Shirley
Surge Protection
The Surface Dwellers
SurfWatch Parental Aid
Surgically Enhanced
Suspicious Stains
Swallowing Shit
Swampfoot
Swarming Midgets
The Swarthy Rogues
Sweaty Thigh Master
The Swedish Pregnancy Team
Sweeps Week
The Sweet Life
Sweet Potato Pickup
Sweetbelly Freakdown
Sweetesque
Swim Herschel Swim
Swimming Maggot Frog
Swing Set
The Swing Set
Swinging Hepcats
The Swinging Pendulums
Switzerland, My Light Is On
Swiss Army
The Symbiotes
Symbol Boy
Sylvia Your Fax Didn't Go Through
Sympathetic Vibrations
Syndication
Synthetic Future
Synthetic Ned
System Error

T

TBA
T. Ease
T.H.U.D.
Tabun
Tacklebox Vacuum Woes
Taco Trash
Taipan
Take It Outside
Take That
Take-Out Menu
Take Out Or Eat In
Taken For Granite
Taken Out
Taking The Cake
Taking Umbrage
Talk Show Circuit
Talking Dog
Talking Statues
Tammy's Clothes
Tanning Juice
Tantalizing Apple
Tapeworm Enchilada
Tarot Parlor
Tastes Like Chicken
The Tasty Floaters
The Taters
Tattletale

Tautology
Tax And Spend
Tax Bracket
Tax That Ass
Tea Bag
Teacher Kickers
Tearin' It Up
Tears And Vomit
Technical Difficulties
Techno-Doze
Teen Frenzy
Teenage Mutant Milton Berle
The Teeny Weenies
Telephone Pole Of Enlightenment
Television Twig
Tell Me Everything
Tell Us About Your Mother
Temporal Disturbance
Temporary Compost
Ten Best
Ten Is My Un-Favorite Number
Ten Minute Divorce
Ten Thousand Tons Of Cyanide
Tender Chicken
The Tendrils
Tense Moment
The Teratogens
Terminal Boredom
Terminal Enid
Terminal Hold
Terminal Illness
Terra Plane
Terrific Disposal Unit
Test Range
Tetrahedron
Tetral
Texas Toast
The That
That Away
That Band
That Band That Sucks
That Warm Electric Feeling
That Was Close
That Which Ensues
That'll Do It
That's Gotta Hurt
That's Not Him
That's-a Nice-a Donut
Theoretically
There's No Law Against It
Thermal Exhaustion
These Last Few Days
The Thetans
They Might Be Clients
Thickening Drip
Thin Ice
The Thing Is
Third Triumvirate
This Day And Age
This End Up
This Is A Pen, I Am A Boy
This Just In
This Name Is Never Spoken
This Picture Of A Phallus Costs Ten Yen
This Place Sucks
This Space Available
This Steak Is Burnt
Thomas Guide
Thong And A Push Bike
Thorncopter

Those Amazing Norwegians
Those Obnoxious Aliens
Three Blind Mics
Three Chord Monty
Three Dweebs
The Three Fates
Three-Finger Salute
Three Guys With Hair
Three Men And Another Man
Three Meter Peter
Three Steps To Kevin
Three Wishes
Three-Stiff Trunk
Thriving On Alarm
Throw Rocks At That Man
Thunderbroom
Ticket To Floss
Ticketmonster
Tidbit Basket
Tie Me Down And Spit
Tied For Fifth
Tiger Snake Dance
Tigertail
Tile Cleaner
Tile Experts
Time And A Half
Time Code
Time Daughter
Time Delay
Time For A Pastry
Time For Bed
Time Series
Tin Maiden
Tin Sin
The Tinctures
The Tinkles
Tinkling Treacle
Tiny Classified Ads
Tiny Star Bat
Tipping The Skiff
The Tips
Tirade
Titanics In Spandex
To Be Announced
To Darren, On His Nineteenth Birthday
To Hell With That
To Staple The Hens
To The Cleaners
To The Core
To Wit
Toadal Recall
The Toast Is On Fire
Toaster Oven Fruitcake
Toasty-Warm Ampersand
Today's My Super Spaceout Day
Toe Cleavage
Toe-Sucking Duchess
Toenail Fungus
Toilet Bowls
Tokamak
Tomato Soup
Tomato Toss
Tommy's Naughty Secret
Tommyrot
Toneburst
Tongue In Grove
Tonguedart Olympians
Tonight
Tonka
The Tonsil Chunks
Took This
Tookesbury Omelet Revue
The Top 10
Top And Bottom
Top Darts
Top Heavy

Top Secretary
The Toppings
Topsoil
Tora! Tora! Tora!
Tori! Tori! Tori!
Torment
Torn Between Two Lovers By Mary McGregor
The Tortillas You Wanted
Torture Club
Torture Dog
The Tossers
The Total Doorknobs
Total Gravity
The Total Population Of China
Touch And Concern
Touch My Kidney
The Touch Tones
The Touchables
Toupeed Head
Townsville Sons
Toxic Chaos
Toxic Crayons
Toxoid
Tra La La
Trachodon Ball
Tractor Pull Follies
Tractor Shop
Tragedy Of Youth
Train Wreck
The Transactions
Transbay Tube
Transmute
Trapezoid
Tree Farm
The Trickster Gods
Trigger Finger
Trinitrotoluene
Trioxane Delight
Triple Bypass
The Triple Integrals
Triplicate
Trite Untrue
Trophy Wife
Tropic Of Cancer
Tropic Of Crap
Trotsky Lives
Troubleseekers
Trucial States
The Trucking Life
True Stories Of The Bozo Patrol
True To Form
Trump Agate
Truth Ache
Truth Mercilessly Crushed by Beauty
Try Again
Tubesteak Marina
Tucked In
The Tummies
Tummy Rumbles
Tumpies
The Tumult
Tuneless Humming
Tunnel Ram
Tunnel Vision
Tupperware Tag Team
Turbo Diesel
Turbo Philosophorum
Turkey Makes Me Sleepy
Turn Of The Century
Turn To Dust
Turtle Cake
Turtle Moon
The Turtlenecks
Twatwurst
Tweezer
Twin Paradox

Twin Skippy
Two Chunks Of Sodium And A Cracker
Two Lions Respecting Each Other
Two Men At A Urinal
Two Nuns Go Into A Bar
Two Slow Breaths
Two Tens For A Five
Two Thumbs Up
Two-Fisted Elliot
Tyne And Wear

U

The U-Boats
The Ugly Kissers
Ugly Mean Sad People
The Ugly Pugs
Uh-Oh
The Ukulele Joy Choir
Ulan Bator
The Ultimate Waffle
Ultrachrist
Uluating Ungulates
Umbrella Man
The Umlauts
The Unbelievable Truth
Unbreakable Comb
The Uncalled Four
The Uncarved Block
The Uncertain Radicals
Uncle Bobby's Wild Oats
Uncle Charley's Funk Tarts

Uncle Grunty's Unt-Unt Fizz
Uncle Jesse's Truck
Uncle Puppy
Uncouth 28-Sided Figure
Under Cromwell
Under The Eight Ball
Under The Hourglass
Under The Knife
Under The L
The Underachievers
The Undergrads
Underground Restaurant
The Understanders
Undecided Alternative Blues
Undescended Testicle
Undesirable Symptoms
Undo
Undulating Freeways
Undulatory Nightmare
Unearthly Child
Unemployment
The Unholy Band From The Holy Land
The Unidentified
Unified Field Theory
Uniform Inconsistency
Unimind
Unintentional Ed
The Union
Unique Band Identifier
Unique Process
Universal Orgiastic Picnic
Universal Symptoms
Universal Tongue
Unleaded Milk
The Unleashed
Unmasculine
Unnamables

Uno Mas Cerveza Por Favor
Untalented Poseurs
The Untold Story
Unvoiced Vowels
Unwanted Advice
Up The Wazoo
Up To Date
Up Yours
The Uppity Bump Jazz
Upward
Urban Biscuit Jouster
Urban Persuasion
Urchin Flake
Urinal Cake Department Manager
Urine Analysis
Urine Specimen
Urn Zone
USA-A-OK
Usage Notes
Use As Directed
Use No Hooks
User Fees
Uterus Crew
Uvula Glue

Van Gogh's Ear
Van Goo
Van Or Astrovan?
Vandenheed
Vanishing Act
Various Artists
The Varmints
The Vast Void Of Empty Nothingness
Vaticanallica
Vector Analysis
Vegan's Beef Nightmare
The Vegas Cocks
Vegetarian Butcher
Vehement Denial
Velveeta Underground
Velvet Bells
Velvet Crunch
Venusian Bind
Verbatim
Vermin Paladins
Vermious
Verse Vica
Vertebrate Head Organizer
Vertical Lines And The Price You Pay
Vertical Smile
Very Happy
The Veto Brothers
Vibrolush
Vice Presidents Of The United States Of America
Vicious Circle
The Vicissitudes Of Time
Victims Aid Society
Video Killed The Radio Shack
Vinaigrette Dread
Vincent Van Go
Vinegar Bible
Violent Constituency

V

Vacation Bible School
Vaccination Hallucination
Valiant Uncles

Violent Solutions To Sexual Megaproblems
The Virgin-Whore Complex
Visceral Bishop
The Visigoths
Visiting Oligarchy
The Visitor From Porlock
Visual Spacek
Vitamin P
Vituperous Earl
Vlad Tepes
Voice Of America
Voice Of Raisin
Voice Of Reason
Void Where Prohibited
Volcanic Sluts
Volcano Orphanage
Volume 1
Voluminous Dwarf
The Voluptuous Horror Of Abe Vigoda
Vomit Suppressor
Voodoo Economics
Voodoo Love Modems
Voodoo School
Vortex
The Vouchers
Vowel Movement
Vulgarity Sucks
Vulture Maiden

W

Wacky Neighbor
Waco Bell
Waging War
Wait Just A Gol-Durned Minute
Walk Don't Walk
Walla Walla Bing Bang
The Wankers
Wanton Carnage
The Wapners
Warm And Forbidding
The Warm Afterglows
Warm Dry Dog Nose
The Warm-Up Band
Warrior Princess
Watchers Of The Skies
Waste Of Time
Wave View
Wax On Wax Off
Waxahachie Widows
Waxworks
Way To Go
Wayward Slugs
We Are Everywhere
We Couldn't Spell It
We Couldn't Tell You
We Don't Know Yet
We Have A Winner
We Have Frogs Legs
We Have Podlike Feet
We Have Ways Of Making You Rock
We Haven't Heard Of You Either
We Mean Business
We Of The Never Never

We Want Our Mail, Not the Tacos
We Who Are Not Us
We Will Not Be Here
We're Here For You
We're Kidding
We're No Elvis
Wearing Barrels
Weather Mirror
The Week In Review
Weekend Numismatist
Weekly World News
Weevil Board
Weigh Station
Weight Before Cooking
Weird Al Reykjavik
Weird Interior
Weird Noises
The Welcome Strangers
The Well I'm Sure I Left It There Yesterday Band
Well...
Wendy, I Can Fly
Wesley's Gonna Get It
Wet Cat
Wet Cement
Wet Toga Contest
Wet Tooth
Wet Wedge
Wet Wet Soggy
Wetland Boomtown
The What
What A Woman
What About The Marxists?
What About Torture
What Happened
What In Sam Hill
What It Is
What Long Distance Plan Are You Using?
What Was Once Shocking Is Now Boring
What Women Want
What You Are About To See
What's Your Product?
Wheatbox
Wheel Head Cross
Wheel-O
When Did Jake Arrive?
When Pigs Fly
Where Is The Ceiling?
Where Is Theo Being Held?
Which Means What
Which Part?
Whined and Dined
Whiplash Lawsuit
Whirling Butt Cherries
Whiskers Of Impotence
Whisper-Quiet
Whistler's Mother
White Flour Children
White Ford Bronco
White Thrash
Whiteacre
Who Carries The Organ
Who Killed The Cat
Who The Hell Are You?
Who's Holdin'
Who's Your Tailor? I Love Your Outfit!
Wholesale Piecemeal
Whom The Gods Destroy
Whup-Ass Transfusion
Whut Thuh
Why Don't You Wash That Thing
Wicked Chicken
Wicked Fudge Lovers
Widdershins
Wide Load

The Widgets
Widows 95
The Wife's Ruining It
Wild Card
Wild Kingdom After Dark
Wile E. Peyote
Will Play Songs For Food
Will Work For Food
William Shatner's Pants
Windows 1895
Windows For Shitheads
Winds Of Aeolus
The Winner Is
The Wire Twists
Wish I Was Cool
Wish Upon A Lousy Star
Witch Baby
Witch Mountain Standard Time
With Friends And Blowers
With Impunity
With One Spring He Was Free
Without Delay
Witty Wit
Wizard Of Odds
Wolverine Blues
The Womenfolk
Won't Do
Wonder Troubles
Wonderful Band Name
Wonderful Wino
Wood Pulp Product
Woodrow Nixon
Woodstock Degeneration
The Woodtones
Wookie Lust
The Words
Worf And The Stone Kittens
The Work Of God

Working For Scale
Working Title
World Of Fish
The World Of Tomorrow
World Teacup
World's Toughest Rodeo
Worm Slice
Wormhole
Worst Business Bureau
Worst Of All Possible Worlds
Worst To First
Wotsit Doodah
Wowie Zowie
Wrasslin' A Greased Hawg
Wreckcreation
Wrecked 'Em
The Write-Offs
The Wrong Crowd

X

X Is For Xine
X-Cow
X-File Manager
The X-Rays
X-Wing Cockroach
X. Lax And The Loose Load
Xenophobic Revue
Xeroxing My Mother's Shoes
XXX-Files
Xylomorphic Treehuggers In The Armpit Of An Angry Fascist
Xyphoid Prostrate

Y

Ya Blokos!
Yackity
Yahweh Or The Highway
Yahweh Prison
Yard Sale And The Good Deal
Yarmulke Chinstrap
The Yaws
Ye Olde Megamalle
Yeah You
Yellow #5
Yellow, Black And Teal
The Yellow Pages
Yellow With Age
The Yellowstone National Variety Revue And Livery Emporium
Yeltsin Matrushka
Yet Another Beatles Tribute Band
Yeti Again
Yikes
Yog Sothoth Neblod Ska
Yoko Ono's Ass
You Are Evil And Must Be Destroyed
You Bastard
You Dance
You Did What With My Emmy Award?
You Don't Say
You Drive, I'll Sleep
You Gotty Squatty
You May Already Be A Winner
You Pick 'Em
You Shall Be Destroyed
You Should Know
You'll Like It
You'll Shit In Terror
You're Half The Man Your Mother Was
You're Next
You're Not Invited
You're Soaking In It
You're The Man
Young Queen
The Young Socialist
The Young'uns
Your Basic Band
Your Chances Of Being Killed
Your Cordial Hosts
Your Fiesta
Your Mileage May Vary
Your Mom
Your Name Here
Your New Neighbors
Your Tax Dollars At Work
Your Worst Nightmare
Yours In Christ
Yummy Juice
Yummytree
Yuppie Chow
Yuppie In A Coma
Yurt Of The Unwashed Shepherd

Z

Z Is Last
Zag, Yag And The Marlboro Man
Zany Marxist Tycoon
Zeitgeistbusters
Zen For Primates
Zen Frequency
Zero-Bias Tone Arm
Zero Chance In A Sandwich
Zero Golf
Zero Point One Tolerance
Zero Sum
Zero Truth
Zeus Pistol
Zinc Cardigan
Zircon Coffeehouse
Zombie Lake
Zombie Zither
Zoo Story
Zsa Zsa
Zubin And The Metaphysicians
Zwieback Of Zymurgy
The Zymotics
Zymurgy And Misogyny

Once upon a time there was a band known 'round here simply as "The Band With No Name." Kind-hearted souls from near and far donated band name suggestions, until one day, Juicebox was born. Happily, they rocked ever after.

If you're still fishing for your own perfect band name, give The Long List a try.

Updated: 11/29/96.
Query? Bizarre tale? Email us.